Adolescent Dating Violence

About the Authors

Kelli S. Franco, PhD, is a licensed psychologist, assistant professor, and postdoctoral pediatric psychology training director with Baylor College of Medicine at CHRISTUS Children's in San Antonio, TX. Her clinical specialties include adolescent concerns, trauma-related disorders, and mood disorders. Dr. Franco's research addresses pediatric trauma, dating violence prevention, and risky adolescent behavior.

Emily F. Rothman, ScD, is a social epidemiologist, professor and chair of occupational therapy at Boston University, MA. Her research focuses on dating and sexual violence prevention, pornography, and autism.

Jeff R. Temple, PhD, is a professor, licensed psychologist, and the associate dean for clinical research for the School of Behavioral Health Sciences at the University of Texas Health Science Center at Houston, TX, where he also holds the Betty and Rose Pfefferbaum Chair in Child Mass Trauma and Resilience. As the founding director of the Texas Violence and Injury Prevention Research Center, his research focuses on the prevention of interpersonal violence, with a particular focus on adolescent dating violence.

Advances in Psychotherapy – Evidence-Based Practice

Series Editor
Danny Wedding, PhD, MPH, Professor Emeritus, University of Missouri–Saint Louis, MO

Associate Editors
Jonathan S. Comer, PhD, Professor of Psychology and Psychiatry, Director of Mental Health Interventions and Technology (MINT) Program, Center for Children and Families, Florida International University, Miami, FL

Kenneth E. Freedland, PhD, Professor of Psychiatry and Psychology, Washington University School of Medicine, St. Louis, MO

J. Kim Penberthy, PhD, ABPP, Professor of Psychiatry & Neurobehavioral Sciences, University of Virginia, Charlottesville, VA

Linda C. Sobell, PhD, ABPP, Professor, Center for Psychological Studies, Nova Southeastern University, Ft. Lauderdale, FL

David A. Wolfe, our esteemed Past Associate Editor, was the responsible scientific editor for this volume.

The basic objective of this series is to provide therapists with practical, evidence-based treatment guidance for the most common disorders seen in clinical practice – and to do so in a reader-friendly manner. Each book in the series is both a compact "how-to" reference on a particular disorder for use by professional clinicians in their daily work and an ideal educational resource for students as well as for practice-oriented continuing education.

The most important feature of the books is that they are practical and easy to use: All are structured similarly and all provide a compact and easy-to-follow guide to all aspects that are relevant in real-life practice. Tables, boxed clinical "pearls," marginal notes, and summary boxes assist orientation, while checklists provide tools for use in daily practice.

Continuing Education Credits

Psychologists and other healthcare providers may earn five continuing education credits for reading the books in the *Advances in Psychotherapy* series and taking a multiple-choice exam. This continuing education program is a partnership of Hogrefe Publishing and the National Register of Health Service Psychologists. Details are available at https://www.hogrefe.com/us/cenatreg

The National Register of Health Service Psychologists is approved by the American Psychological Association to sponsor continuing education for psychologists. The National Register maintains responsibility for this program and its content.

Advances in Psychotherapy – Evidence-Based Practice, Volume 56

Adolescent Dating Violence

Kelli S. Franco
Baylor College of Medicine at CHRISTUS Children's, San Antonio, TX

Emily F. Rothman
Boston University College of Health & Rehabilitation Sciences,
Sargent College Occupational Therapy, Boston University, Boston, MA

Jeff R. Temple
School of Behavioral Health Sciences, UTHealth Houston, Houston, TX

Library of Congress Cataloging in Publication information for the print version of this book is available via the Library of Congress Marc Database under the Library of Congress Control Number 2025947264

Library and Archives Canada Cataloguing in Publication
Title: Adolescent dating violence / Kelli S. Franco, Baylor College of Medicine at CHRISTUS
    Children's, San Antonio, TX, Emily F. Rothman, Boston University College of Health &
    Rehabilitation Sciences, Sargent College Occupational Therapy, Boston University, Boston, MA,
    Jeff R. Temple, School of Behavioral Health Sciences, UTHealth Houston, Houston, TX.
Names: Franco, Kelli S., author. | Rothman, Emily F., author. | Temple, Jeff R., author
Series: Advances in psychotherapy--evidence-based practice ; v. 56.
Description: Series statement: Advances in psychotherapy--evidence-based practice ; volume 56. |
    Includes bibliographical references.
Identifiers: Canadiana (print) 20250280876 | Canadiana (ebook) 20250283611 | ISBN 9780889374195
    (softcover) | ISBN 9781616764197 (PDF) | ISBN 9781613344194 (EPUB)
Subjects: LCSH: Adolescent psychotherapy. | LCSH: Dating violence. | LCSH: Dating violence—
    Prevention. | LCSH: Victims of dating violence. | LCSH: Abused teenagers. | LCSH: Violence in
    adolescence. | LCSH: Teenagers—Abuse of.
Classification: LCC RJ503 .F73 2025 | DDC 616.89/140835—dc23

Publishing Offices
USA: Hogrefe Publishing Corporation, 44 Merrimac St., Newburyport, MA 01950
Phone 978 255 3700; E-mail customersupport@hogrefe.com
EUROPE: Hogrefe Publishing GmbH, Merkelstr. 3, 37085 Göttingen, Germany
Phone +49 551 99950 0, Fax +49 551 99950 111; E-mail publishing@hogrefe.com

Sales & Distribution
USA: Hogrefe Publishing, Customer Services Department, 30 Amberwood Parkway, Ashland, OH 44805
Phone 800 228 3749, Fax 419 281 6883; E-mail customersupport@hogrefe.com
UK: Hogrefe Ltd, Hogrefe House, Albion Place, Oxford, OX1 1QZ
Phone +44 186 579 7920; E-mail customersupport@hogrefe.co.uk
EUROPE: Hogrefe Publishing, Merkelstr. 3, 37085 Göttingen, Germany
Phone +49 551 99950 0, Fax +49 551 99950 111; E-mail publishing@hogrefe.com

Other Offices
CANADA: Hogrefe Publishing Corporation, 82 Laird Drive, East York, Ontario, M4G 3V1
SWITZERLAND: Hogrefe Publishing, Länggass-Strasse 76, 3012 Bern

ISBN 978-0-88937-419-5 (print) · ISBN 978-1-61676-419-7 (PDF) · ISBN 978-1-61334-419-4 (EPUB)
https://doi.org/10.1027/00419-000

Contents

1

Description

Adolescent dating violence (ADV) is a public health crisis that affects 10s of thousands of adolescents and emerging adults each year, sometimes with deadly consequences. In many instances, though, dating violence goes unrecognized by mental health professionals, caregivers, teachers, and friends of those victimized or perpetrating the aggressive behavior. Given its prevalence and the severity of the impact on those affected, professionals need to know how to (1) recognize the signs that a young person is in an abusive or unhealthy dating relationship, (2) evaluate the problem in the context of other co-occurring disorders, and (3) pursue referral and treatment options that protect youths and promote their well-being.

This book will present an overview of ADV, diagnostic guidelines, and methods of assessing youths for victimization and perpetration; explain present-day theories about why ADV occurs; and review referral and intervention options. Although dating violence can be experienced by anyone who has romantic relationships or intimate partners – including older persons and adults – we will focus on youths aged 10 to 24 years, for three reasons.

First, individuals in this age group are most likely to experience dating violence. Second, adolescents and emerging adults are developmentally analogous, including possessing similar risk (e.g., binge drinking) and protective (e.g., prosocial friends) factors for experiencing ADV. Third, the methods of identifying and responding to cases of dating violence in adolescent and emerging adult phases of development generally differ from those in more established (often cohabiting) relationships. Driven by mounting evidence, we take the perspective that victims of dating violence may be of any gender and that dating violence can occur in any type of relationship (i.e., heterosexual or same-sex).

Also reflective of evidence in the field, we take the stance that dating violence victimization and perpetration can be compounded by societal-level discrimination and oppression. Our intersectional approach acknowledges that people with less power in society (e.g., women; gender and sexual minorities; Black, Indigenous, and other people of color; people living in poverty; disabled people, (im)migrants or non–English speakers; among others) can face multiple additional barriers to receiving adequate help when they are victimized or when they perpetrate dating violence.

Our goal for this book is twofold. We will relay the findings of the most recent research on ADV, and we will provide tools, resources, and recommendations that behavioral health practitioners can use in the field. Above all, it is our hope that the too-often-overlooked phenomenon of dating violence will be seen, understood, and responded to with the deep level of concern that is warranted. Far too many cases of ADV have been ignored or minimized by well-meaning people who have bought into the idea that "puppy love" is inconsequential or that aggressive behavior by boys is acceptable because "boys will be boys."

Dispelling myths: Victims aren't to blame, and perpetrators can be treated effectively

Other pervasive myths about dating violence are that victims are at least partially to blame, for reasons ranging from how flirtatious or sexually active they are, to whether they have witnessed interparental violence at home, to whether they drink alcohol or use other illicit substances. None of these factors explain responsibility for dating violence perpetration, and none should cloud the judgment of mental health clinicians whose goal is to treat dating violence as an adolescent health issue equally as important to safety and health as eating disorders, mood disorders, or personality disorders. A final myth that we wish to dispel is the widely held belief that perpetrators of dating violence cannot be treated. We have every confidence that clinicians and other youth-serving providers can make a significant difference in the lives of young people. Education about the topic of dating violence, as well as recommended practices for preventing, counseling, and referring those affected, is the first step.

1.1   Terminology

Historically, when clinicians and researchers first began to study the phenomenon of violence in youth dating relationships, they generally referred to it as *teen dating violence* (TDV). While the term TDV is still commonly used in the literature and popular press, there is increasing use of the terms *adolescent dating violence* (ADV) and *adolescent relationship abuse*. These last two terms are more inclusive and encompass a wider age range. *Dating violence* is often used to refer to any abuse in emerging and young adult dating (nonmarital) relationships. The terms *intimate partner violence* (hereafter referred to as IPV) and *domestic violence* are generally used by researchers and practitioners when discussing violence in cohabiting or married adult relationships.

ADV includes multiple abuse types, can be one- or two-sided, and varies in severity and impact

Adolescent dating violence (ADV), our preferred term, refers to actual or threatened physical violence, sexual assault, stalking, psychological and/or emotional abuse, or any combination thereof (all defined below). Abusive acts can occur between dating partners of any gender or sexual identity. ADV can be unidirectional (i.e., one dating partner is violent toward the other) or bidirectional (i.e., both dating partners violent toward each other). In the latter case, it is important to note that bidirectional or mutual violence does not necessarily mean that the violence is equal in frequency or severity (Temple et al., 2005). Some individuals may use infrequent or minor aggression or self-defensive violence in a relationship, but nevertheless experience powerlessness.

Another linguistic issue is whether to call a person who experiences ADV a "survivor" or a "victim." The word "survivor" is often used by community agencies and is a well-intentioned positive reframe on the abusive event and recovery process. The word "victim" is typically used in research and criminal justice settings, and given the short- and long-term consequences of abuse, this is the term we use in this volume. Similarly, the term "perpetrator" refers to individuals who enact violence against their dating partner. Embracing a trauma-informed approach necessitates that we acknowledge many perpetrators are also victims of interpersonal violence (Ybarra et al., 2016), and stigmatizing, reductionist labels such as "perpetrator" perpetuate counterproductive myths about the etiology and course of ADV. However, for clarity and brevity and with some misgivings, we use the terms perpetrator and victim throughout this volume. We hope that clinicians will embrace trauma-informed, people-first language such as "youths who use/experience violence."

> **Terms like "victim" and "perpetrator" aid clarity, but people-first phrasing is preferred**

1.2   Definitions

The construct of ADV is defined very similarly to how researchers and clinicians in the field of violence prevention define adult IPV. Importantly, the *Diagnostic and Statistical Manual of Mental Disorders,* 5th edition, text revision (DSM-5-TR; American Psychiatric Association [APA], 2022) definition of IPV requires the presence of a specific type of abusive act (i.e., physical, sexual, or psychological aggression), and that act must have had a significant injurious impact or had a high potential for such an impact (e.g., threatening a partner with a gun; see Heyman et al., 2015, for complete definitions of IPV in DSM-5-TR and ICD-11). In other words, according to the DSM-5-TR definition, if a person were to slap or shove their partner and it did not cause fear, injury, or have a high potential for causing fear or injury, it would not qualify as partner violence. An exception is made for sexual abuse. This definition is consistent with the definition provided by the US Centers for Disease Control and Prevention (CDC), which posits that "IPV can vary in how often it happens and how severe it is. It can range from one episode of violence that could have lasting impact to chronic and severe episodes over multiple years" (CDC, 2022).

One important consideration when it comes to defining ADV, specifically, is that adolescents often engage in flirtatious joking, rough-housing, or horseplay (i.e., a playful swat on the shoulder, grabbing an arm to start a wrestling match) that could be misattributed as violence (Hamby, 2017). However, it is important that clinicians assess whether both individuals consider the rough-housing consensual and noninjurious. Similarly, some adolescents and young adults may choose to engage in rough sex (e.g., sex that includes spanking or hair pulling). Without explicit and noncoerced consent negotiated in advance, rough sex may be experienced as – and may qualify as – assault.

Another challenge in recognizing ADV is that unlike marital and cohabiting adult relationships, "dating" relationships can be challenging to define. Teenage relationships are often characterized by shorter duration than adult intimate partnerships, a "churning" on-again-off-again nature, a preliminary "talking stage" with vague commitment boundaries, and "friends with benefits" arrangements in which sexual and romantic intimacy can occur in the absence of clear relationship labels or terms of conduct (Manning et al., 2014).

US law is also vague about what, precisely, should count as a dating relationship. According to the US federal Violence Against Women Act (34 US Code § 12291), the term "dating violence" means (A) violence committed by a person who is or has been in a social relationship of a romantic or intimate nature with the victim; and (B) where the existence of such a relationship is determined based on a consideration of the following factors: (1) length of the relationship, (2) type of relationship, and (3) frequency of interaction between the persons involved in the relationship (Congressional Research Service, 1993). Because the length and type of relationship are undefined, discretion is left to individual judges to decide whether two individuals who have spent as little as one night together (i.e., have "hooked up") have been in a dating relationship or not.

Consistent with the CDC's definition, we conceptualize ADV to include acts of physical, sexual, or psychological violence occurring with a current or former romantic partner (broadly defined). These acts can occur in person or via electronic means. Below we provide specific definitions and examples for each subtype of ADV. An individual event may represent one, multiple, or all subtypes (e.g., a sexual assault at gun point during which the victim is verbally insulted would be considered physically, sexually, and psychologically violent, whereas a single degrading comment during a verbal conflict reflects "only" psychological violence).

1.2.1   Physical ADV

Consistent with the definition of adult IPV, *physical ADV* refers to any attempt or act to physically hurt, injure, or harm a dating partner (of the opposite or same sex). Examples include hits, punches, kicks, shoves, scratches, thrown objects, or threats of physical harm. In the research literature, threats using a firearm or other weapon are commonly considered an act of physical ADV (as opposed to emotional or psychological ADV) due to substantial risk of physical harm.

About Homicide

Seven percent of youth homicides (of individuals aged 11–24) in the US are classified as intimate partner homicides

An understudied and horrific phenomenon is intimate partner homicide of adolescents. Data show 7% of all youth homicides (of individuals ages 11 to 24) in the United States are classified as intimate partner homicides. Of these intimate partner homicides, the staggering majority of victims (90%) are female, and firearms are the most common mechanism of injury (Adhia et al., 2019). Youths appear particularly at risk for deadly conduct with dating partners in the context of teenage pregnancy and easy access to firearms (Bender et al., 2021). Not only is additional research and attention needed to understand and prevent youth fatalities, but these tragedies also remind us that minimizing the seriousness of ADV and considering it immature adolescent "drama" or "angst" can have deadly consequences.

1.2.2 Sexual ADV

Sexual ADV refers to acts in which one dating partner forces, coerces, or attempts to engage in sexual acts or touching when the other partner does not or cannot consent. Acts of sexual ADV that qualify can include kissing, groping, rubbing, or fondling that is against the expressed wishes of the dating partner and causes considerable distress, or coercing a partner to send sexually explicit images or engage in rough sex. This term also encompasses acts of criminally recognized sexual assault and rape. Additionally, sexual ADV includes behaviors that control the (non)use of contraceptives or condoms without mutual consent (sometimes referred to as *reproductive coercion*), "stealthing" during which a dating partner secretly removes a condom during sex, the nonconsensual dissemination of sexually explicit images, sending unwanted sexual images or texts, and creating deepfake pornography of a partner. Note that sexual exploitation of minors and related human trafficking, although potentially perpetrated by a dating partner, is beyond the scope of this volume.

1.2.3 Psychological ADV

Psychological ADV, also commonly referred to as *emotional ADV or verbal ADV*, refers to the use of verbal or nonverbal communication with the intent to harm a dating partner mentally or emotionally and/or exert control. This may include nonaccidental acts such as berating, disparaging, degrading, or humiliating the victim; interrogating the victim; restricting the victim's ability to come and go freely; limiting the victim's contact with family or friends; monitoring or controlling a victim's use of technology; controlling a victim's clothing or other presentation of appearance; verbally threatening the victim or implying future harm of the victim or things or people that the victim cares about; or trying to make the victim think that they are mentally ill. Some researchers also differentiate acts of relational abuse from psychological violence. Acts of relational abuse can include spreading unflattering or untrue rumors about a dating partner, attempts to turn a victim's friends against them, or other acts of social manipulation to harm a victim. Throughout this volume, we incorporate acts of relational abuse under the umbrella of psychological abuse.

Psychological ADV may be realized as psychological distress; a victim's fear interfering with their ability to carry out their employment-related activities, education, religious faith, necessary medical or mental health services, or contact with family and friends; and stress-related somatic symptoms that interfere with healthy functioning.

About Stalking

There has been some debate about whether *stalking* counts as psychological ADV or physical ADV, or is a unique form unto itself. Stalking is a pattern of repeated, unwanted attention and contact from a partner that causes fear or concern for one's safety. Among adolescents, stalking often takes the form of tracking a dating partner's whereabouts (particularly through electronic means), requiring passwords or unrestricted access to their partner's devices and social media, or physically following their partner. Constantly calling or messaging a partner is also considered a form of controlling, and stalking-like, behavior.

About Cyber Abuse

Cyber ADV involves technnology-based abuse, often tied to traditional ADV, like monitoring or threats

Research continues to deliberate whether *cyber ADV* is a unique subtype of ADV or a vehicle through which ADV occurs. Studies show that cyber victimization and perpetration are linked with traditional in-person psychological, sexual, and physical ADV involvement (Sargent et al., 2016; Temple et al., 2016; Zweig et al., 2013). Common methods in which technology is used to abuse a dating partner include texting as a means to monitor a partner's activities, looking at their messages without their knowledge, leaving threatening text messages for them, and posting insulting content about them.

1.3   Epidemiology

How common is ADV? Researchers typically measure either lifetime or recent (e.g., past 6 months, past year) experiences with ADV by considering lifetime exposure or more. Importantly, assessing recent/current and lifetime prevalence of ADV offer their own benefits and challenges. With respect to the former, we can estimate new cases of ADV and whether interventions or enacted policies are having a positive effect (or, conversely, if rates of ADV are increasing due to a concomitant increase in other behaviors, e.g., substance use). Measuring recent experiences with ADV, as opposed to lifetime exposure, is also less susceptible to recall bias. However, lifetime prevalence helps us understand the proportion of people to ever be impacted by ADV – important, given the potential lifetime consequences of ADV victimization and perpetration.

1.3.1   Recent Exposure to ADV

According to US nationally representative data from the Youth Risk Behavior Survey, 10% of high school-attending girls and nearly 7% of boys reported experiencing physical dating violence in the past year (Center for Disease Control and Prevention, 2021). In addition, 15% of girls and 4% of boys reported experiencing sexual dating violence in the past year (Center for Disease Control and Prevention, 2021). Given that as of 2021, there were more than 43 million adolescents in the US between the ages of 10 and 19 years (US Census Bureau, 2022), there are likely between 3 million and 7 million cases of dating abuse victimization each year across the country.

As a point of comparison, in a nationally representative sample of US adults aged 18–59 years, 6% of women and 5% of men reported experiencing physical, sexual, or stalking partner violence victimization in the past year, suggesting that dating violence is more common among adolescents than it is among adults who are in intimate relationships (Smith et al., 2018). In fact, 25% of all US women who experience partner violence victimization in their lifetime report that their first victimization experience was when they were less than 18 years old, and 71% had their first experience before they were 25 years old (Smith et al., 2018). In contrast, approximately 14% of US male victims of partner violence were first victimized before they turned 18 years old, and 56% were younger than 25 years old (Smith et al., 2018).

1.3.2 Lifetime Prevalence

Taking a broader view than only the past year, and considering lifetime experience with ADV, estimates from the National Survey on Teen Relationships and Intimate Violence (STRiV) suggest that the majority (69%) of 12- to 18-year-olds who have dated in the past year have experienced psychological, physical, or sexual dating abuse at least once in their lifetime. The survey found that as many as 18% of adolescents have experienced physical ADV, and 18% have experienced sexual ADV, at least once (Taylor & Mumford, 2016). The study also found that there is a large degree of overlap between ADV victimization and perpetration. STRiV data suggest that 63% of youths report having perpetrated at least one act of dating abuse in their lifetime and that only 11% of youths have experienced victimization and not perpetrated ADV (Taylor & Mumford, 2016).

A novel method for assessing ADV is to consider the cumulative incidence of ADV in a single cohort – in other words, to assess ADV on a repeated basis over multiple timepoints. Using this approach, which capitalizes on the benefits of recent and lifetime measurement of ADV, Temple and colleagues (2024) found that across 12 years of data collection, 27.3% of participants experienced sexual ADV victimization and 46.1% had experienced physical ADV victimization by age 26. Further, 14.8% had perpetrated at least one act of sexual ADV and 39.0% had perpetrated at least one act of physical ADV against a partner by this age.

1.3.3 Differences by Gender

Historically, researchers in the field of violence prevention have wrestled with questions about whether ADV is disproportionately perpetrated by boys against girls. Today, these questions seem a bit out-of-date, in that they take a binary perspective on gender and leave out nonbinary adolescents altogether. Importantly, emerging evidence suggests that gender minority youths may be at increased risk for ADV victimization (Martin-Storey et al., 2021). While youths of all genders may perpetrate or experience ADV, ADV does appear to be more common and more consequential for female-identifying youths.

That said, some people are surprised to learn that according to self-report data on surveys, girls are just as likely as boys to perpetrate psychological and physical ADV, though less likely to perpetrate sexual ADV (Taylor & Mumford, 2016). However, when men or boys perpetrate ADV against women or girls, their actions appear to be more likely to result in injury, fear, and other tangible harms, such as lost work time or involvement of law enforcement, than when women and girls are the perpetrators (Tharp et al., 2017). In fact, a nationally representative survey of adults between the ages of 18 and 59 found that over the course of their lifetimes, 25% of US women and 11% of US men had experienced partner violence with these types of impacts (Smith et al., 2018) – in other words, women are more than twice as likely to experience fear, injury, and other harms when they are victimized, compared with men.

Thus, while girls and boys may report nearly equivalent rates of shouting, name calling, slapping, and pushing when they complete surveys about ADV behavior (Taylor & Mumford, 2016; Ybarra et al., 2016), most practitioners argue that the typically differing consequences of those actions – which do align with gender – should be taken into consideration. Misogyny, or hatred of women, and social norms that encourage treating women as "less than" in society and in relationships, fuels at least some adolescent perpetrators of dating violence (Reyes et al., 2016). At the same time, focusing too much attention on gender is also a mistake. ADV is important to address and take seriously, no matter the gender of the perpetrator or victim.

1.3.4   Differences by Other Demographic Factors

ADV victimization is more prevalent among older adolescents than younger adolescents (Rothman, Paruk, et al., 2022), presumably in part because older adolescents are more likely to enter into dating and sexual relationships (Carver et al., 2003) their relationships are more likely to be longer term, and they are less likely to be closely monitored by parents.

Whether ADV is more common among youths in racial and ethnic demographic subgroups is not entirely clear (Table 1). Several studies have found that Black, multiracial, and Native American youths are at elevated risk for ADV victimization compared with their White counterparts (Halpern et al., 2001; Rothman & Xuan, 2014). Importantly, the correlation between race/ethnicity and ADV needs to be understood in the context of racism. Numerous factors, including community contexts, societal marginalization, and inequity in health care access may help explain these links (Benson et al., 2004).

Table 1

Prevalence of Physical and Sexual ADV (Referred to Here as TDV) Among High School Students by Demographic Subgroup (N = 13,677)

Characteristic	Physical TDV % (95% CI)	Sexual TDV % (95% CI)
All students	8.2 (7.2–9.4)	8.2 (7.4–9.1)
Sex		
Male	7.0 (5.8–8.4)	3.8 (3.1–4.7)
Female	9.3 (8.0–10.8)	12.6 (11.2–14.2)
Race		
American Indian/Alaskan Native	15.3 (7.1–29.7)	N/A
Asian	6.2 (2.6–14.1)	8.3 (4.1–15.9)
Black	8.2 (6.1–10.8)	6.2 (4.5–8.6)
Native Hawaiian/Pacific Islander	N/A	N/A
White	7.5 (6.4–8.7)	8.1 (6.9–9.6)
Hispanic	8.9 (7.4–10.8)	8.7 (6.9–10.8)
Multiracial	9.5 (6.1–14.4)	10.1 (6.7–15.0)
Grade		
Ninth	5.6 (4.3–7.2)	8.0 (6.4–10.0)
10th	8.1 (6.7–9.9)	7.6 (5.9–9.7)
11th	8.7 (7.3–10.4)	8.4 (6.8–10.4)
12th	9.8 (7.9–12.0)	8.6 (7.2–10.2)
Sexual identity		
Heterosexual	7.2 (6.2–8.3)	6.7 (5.9–7.5)
Gay or lesbian	11.0 (6.3–18.5)	7.2 (3.9–13.0)
Bisexual	13.6 (10.9–16.9)	18.8 (14.3–24.4)
Not sure	16.9 (11.1–24.9)	15.0 (9.5–23.0)

Note. Adapted from National Youth Risk Behavior Survey, Basile et al., 2020. ADV = adolescent dating violence; TDV = teen dating violence.

Emerging research also consistently indicates higher rates of ADV victimization among sexual minority youths compared with their heterosexual peers (Shorey et al., 2018). In fact, being a member of a sexual minority has been shown to increase one's risk for sexual assault victimization fourfold (Porter & Williams, 2011), and sexual minority youths are at especially high risk for sexual assault during their first year of college (Rothman & Silverman, 2007). Why might this be the case? Stigma, homophobia, and oppression can increase vulnerability to violence victimization and make it more difficult to access needed resources (Gillum & DiFulvio, 2012). Moreover, the contents of existing ADV prevention and intervention programs largely address exclusively heterosexual dating relationships, with documented differential effectiveness across heterosexual versus sexual minority groups (Coker et al., 2020).

Rates among justice-involved samples or youths charged with criminal or delinquent status offenses are also elevated, with 36% of females and 65% of males reporting past year physical ADV victimization (Collibee et al., 2022). Justice-involved youths appear to be at elevated risk for ADV victimization and perpetration compared with their peers, at least in part because of the tremendous overlap in risk factors for ADV and general delinquency (Vagi et al., 2013). Shared risk factors include greater exposure to adverse childhood events including community and domestic violence, more affiliation with delinquent peers, earlier initiation of sexual activity, and greater substance misuse.

Prevalence of Dating Violence Has Not Changed Over Time

There is a tendency for the media and others to raise alarm by making claims that certain forms of interpersonal violence are becoming increasingly more common or more prevalent in recent years – perhaps because they think that will help the topic receive the public attention it deserves. The unfortunate truth is that ADV is prevalent, and has been so consistently, for more than 20 years. In fact, there was no change in the prevalence of physical ADV victimization among US high school students from 1999 to 2011 (Rothman & Xuan, 2014), even though there were declines in other forms of violence, such as physical fighting or sexual assault, during that same period of time (Pool et al., 2017). What is more, the rate detected for 1999–2011 is similar to the rate of physical dating violence victimization reported using the same survey tool a few years later in 2014 (Vagi et al., 2015).

While it may be somewhat reassuring to think that the prevalence rate of ADV is not getting worse, the fact that the rate has not decreased substantially at the population level in over 20 years makes it important to invest in prevention and treatment. By responding more effectively to victims and perpetrators, perhaps a downturn trend could emerge in the future.

The fact of no substantial decrease in ADV rate in over 20 years makes it important to invest in prevention and treatment

1.4   Course and Prognosis

1.4.1   Developmental Course: Onset, Peaks, and Revictimization

Risk for the onset of ADV perpetration appears to peak during mid-adolescence for females (ages 15–16) and slightly later (around age 18) for males (Shorey et al., 2017). In addition, there are periods of heightened risk – for example, "red zones" encompass the first 4 months of college where women (especially first-year students) are particularly vulnerable to sexual assault and dating violence (Kimble et al., 2008). Research suggests instances of infidelity or cheating, self-reported jealousy, more frequent disagreements, longer relationship length, and partner continuity also increase the risk for ADV (Giordano et al., 2010; Johnson et al., 2015).

Unfortunately, people who experience ADV victimization appear to be at heightened risk for subsequent victimization as well. In other words, once a person is victimized, that person has a greater-than-average chance of experiencing ADV again in the future (Exner-Cortens et al., 2017; Jouriles et al., 2017). The reason for this revictimization is unclear. On the one hand, it could be that going through an ADV victimization experience causes trauma or another condition that does, indeed, make an individual more vulnerable to unhealthy and controlling dating relationships in the future (Rancher et al., 2019). On the other hand, it could be that there was something earlier in that person's life – for example, experiencing child maltreatment or witnessing interparental violence – that predisposed that person to ADV victimization in their first and subsequent dating relationships. For clients who have experienced ADV, it is important for their autonomy, power, and self-determination to increase their confidence in their ability to navigate relationship choices and steward their own lives successfully.

It is also true that people who perpetrate ADV appear to be more likely to continue to use aggression in future relationships. Longitudinal data points to the stability of perpetration as adolescents develop, with *increases* during late adolescence (Fernández-González et al., 2020; Johnson et al., 2015).

However, based on evidence from related fields, such as substance use, depression, or anxiety, clinicians have reason to feel hopeful that intervention with teenagers who have perpetrated ADV has a good chance of making a meaningful difference, either because psychopathology can be identified and treated, or because adolescents are still developing, and their relationship behavior patterns and styles can be influenced for the better. It is important to acknowledge that in the 1980s–1990s, several longitudinal studies found that early childhood aggression was a strong predictor of future violence perpetration (Walker et al., 2013). However, with increased attention to the importance of addressing adverse childhood experiences, developing trauma-informed care and trauma-informed school models, and implementing social-emotional learning and violence prevention, we may be improving the chances that children who use violence can desist.

1.4.2 Cycle of Abuse Within Dating Relationships

Clinically, the course of an abusive dating relationship is commonly conceptualized in a cycle of four stages, which were originally conceptualized by Walker (2016) and later applied to ADV by Smith and Donnelly (2000) (see Figure 1).

1. **Tension building:** Conflict and tension increase between dating partners. Tension can be evidenced by communication difficulties, expressed emotion, and/or felt hostility, and is often exacerbated by additional

external stressors (e.g., financial, academic pressure). Fear of future violence may develop, met with efforts to placate the perpetrator.

2. **Violent incident:** An act of verbal, emotional, physical, or sexual violence occurs. Anger, blaming, arguing, threats, and intimidation may also occur. This is considered the "flashpoint" explosion when the built tension reaches an apex.

3. **Reconciliation:** Perpetrator may apologize, explain, or excuse their violent behavior. Blaming the victim or denying the occurrence or severity of violence is also common. Perpetrators may use gifts, bribes, and other tools to "prove their love" and negate the violence.

4. **Calm:** The violence incident is "forgotten" or temporarily overlooked. Overt abuse pauses, and partners experience a "honeymoon" phase of increased affection and intimacy.

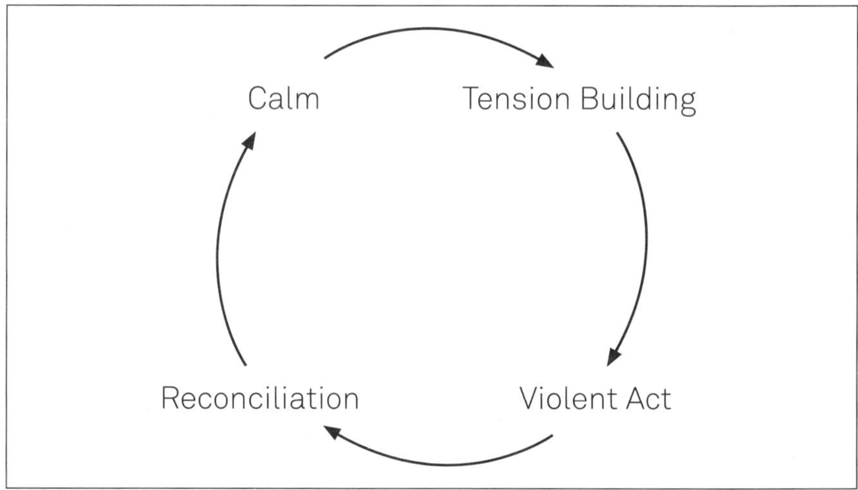

Figure 1
Four stages in cycle of an abusive dating relationship, as originally described by Walker (2016).

The cycle model may oversimplify abuse, yet it can help teens recognize patterns and reconcile calm and violent phases

Valid criticisms of this model include its underlying assumption of unidirectional violence (i.e., a sole victim and a sole perpetrator) and its focus on clear, isolated violent incidents. Thus, persistent occurrence of humiliation, insults, social isolation, or other acts of psychological abuse are not well-captured or addressed. Nevertheless, many providers find the cycle a helpful visual tool when working directly with youths who may be less familiar with abuse definitions and/or may be struggling to reconcile their experience of "honeymoon" calm phases and incidents of violence.

2

Theories and Models

When it comes to ADV, it is useful to understand the leading theories that seek to explain why it occurs. If we know why a particular behavior occurs, we can develop effective and tailored interventions to prevent its occurrence and recurrence. More than 15 theories have been put forward since the early 1900s to explain why people perpetrate partner violence (Rothman, 2018). Note that while a vast majority of these theories were developed and tested on adult IPV, they can and have successfully been applied to ADV. As research has progressed, the field has moved from focusing on explanations that primarily involve individuals' personality traits or history with their family of origin, to considering a wider array of factors, including those that pertain to biology (e.g., stress, traumatic brain injury), peer relationships, institutional factors (e.g., workplace factors, school regulations), neighborhood factors (e.g., disadvantage, collective efficacy), and society (e.g., structural inequity).

In addition to guiding treatment and interventions, theoretical models can be used to explain to adolescents in unhealthy relationships why abuse has happened to them or why they may have perpetrated abuse. Systematic reviews and meta-analyses reveal that many of the same factors that put one at risk for being a victim of ADV are also associated with a higher risk of perpetrating ADV, such as peer influence, normative beliefs about aggression, substance use, depressive symptoms, and more (Spencer et al., 2020, 2021). Moreover, ADV perpetration is a risk marker for ADV victimization and vice versa. Thus, we see that relationship violence is a complex, sometimes reciprocal, and multidetermined experience.

2.1   Background-Situational Model

The *background-situational model* of partner violence perpetration is one of the most well supported by evidence and has been widely used to develop interventions. The model was developed in 1989 by Riggs and O'Leary (1989), who drew upon two established theories of violence perpetration, *Bandura's social learning theory* and *conflict theory*. This model proposes that the way a person behaves in an intimate relationship is caused by a mixture of factors from their distal background and proximal situational factors. For example, background factors, such as experiences of child abuse and neglect or witnessing interparental violence, sibling violence, or peer bullying, appear to shape individuals' propensity for behaving aggressively or impulsively with other people (Cohen et al., 2018). Situational factors, such as using alcohol, having a conflict with a dating partner, or feeling a flash of jealousy, may increase the likelihood that an individual will act aggressively in a particular moment.

Clinicians can utilize this theory with perpetrators of ADV as they discuss their diagnosis and treatment plan, pointing out that their abusive behavior is the result of multiple factors likely from both their past and whatever was going on at the time. For the clinician and the client, this means that focusing exclusively on one factor, such as recovering from the trauma of child abuse, or quitting alcohol, is unlikely to create enough of a change for a person to stop using aggressive behavior in the long term. For behavior to become reliably healthier, it may mean attending to many underlying issues, from their upbringing to their circumstances and choices in present day life.

Focusing exclusively on one factor is unlikely to create a change for a person to stop using aggressive behavior long term

About Anger

An important caveat related to the background-situational model is that while it is true that feeling irritable, angry, or hostile on a given day may be a proximal antecedent of ADV perpetration, and there is evidence to suggest that the trait of hostility is associated with ADV perpetration, the media and general public tend to misunderstand the role of anger in ADV perpetration. Research suggests that "anger is neither a necessary nor sufficient cause" of partner abuse (Crane & Eckhardt, 2013).

Many people who perpetrate ADV may appear angry to others, may perceive that they use aggression because they feel angry, and may even ask for help with anger management. The challenge for the clinician in such situations is to discern which clients can truly benefit from anger management resources in addition to clinical support for the development of healthier intimate partnership skills, and which are using anger as an excuse for behaving in a way that is controlling toward a dating partner. ADV can look like anger from the outside because what is observed is yelling, hitting, or other aggressive behaviors that we tend to associate with conflict and anger.

ADV often appears as anger, but underlying issues usually involve power and control

Sometimes, even for people in an unhealthy relationship, the idea that anger is what is causing the problems may be the easiest cause to imagine. But decades of partner violence advocacy, practice, and research suggest that generalized anger alone is rarely at the heart of the matter. Because the most severe and dangerous forms of partner violence may typically be characterized as one person in the relationship being desperate to have power over and control of the other, assuming that anger management is the primary clinical problem is not recommended. Clinicians may want to assess clients for trait hostility, generalized aggression, and anger management problems, as well as other treatable factors.

2.2   Structural Inequity

Another theory about causes of partner violence pertains to the idea that social inequities can influence how people behave toward intimate partners. According to early feminist theory about partner violence, men may behave abusively toward women in relationships because of societal power imbalances that privilege men (Dobash & Dobash, 1979). A way to paraphrase this theory is that men absorb the idea that they are superior to women, believe that they deserve to command attention and make choices at home or in relationships, expect to be treated with a degree of deference in their partnerships, and enforce their dominant role in the relationship with emotional, physical, sexual, and financial abuse if necessary.

Feminist theory has been challenged to some extent because it fails to explain partner violence in gay and lesbian relationships, or in relationships that include nonbinary or genderqueer individuals, or when women are violent toward men. A broader structural inequity perspective holds that any societal power imbalances that pertain to class, socioeconomic status, employment, race, ethnicity, culture, gender identity, religion, sexual orientation, immigration status, disability status, or age may also play out in individuals' relationships and concentrate decision-making power, or control, in the individual that is part of privileged groups. This does not mean that every relationship that involves differences between two people is inherently unhealthy, and there are many relationships where both partners may belong to one or more of the less-privileged groups.

The key point about structural inequity and intimate relationships is that unless the privileged person puts conscious effort into minimizing societal-level power differences in the relationship, there is a risk that the person with less power will experience marginalization or abuse. For clinicians, considering the intersectional identity of both partners in a dyadic relationship may be relevant for understanding who holds power in the relationship, or who is attempting to gain power in the relationship, and why.

2.3   Neuroscientific Theories of Partner Aggression

Increasing attention has been given to the role of brain injuries in human development and behavior, as well as research on how deficits in verbal ability, cognition, social information processing, and executive function could influence partner aggression. There are several different neurological issues to consider including frontal lobe injury, concussions, intellectual disability, and HPA axis trauma response (McKee & Daneshvar, 2015). Understanding these issues can be useful for the purpose of explaining to clients who may be affected by them how their brain is functioning, which may in turn help them understand how to manage their symptoms or behavior.

Neuroscientists believe that the frontal lobe of the brain plays a major role in self-reflective thinking, perspective taking, organizing complex behavior, attention, and emotional regulation (Séguin, 2009). As such, when the frontal lobe is injured, people may experience changes in personality as a result of decreased capacity for problem solving, which may in turn increase irritability and aggression (Séguin, 2009). Youths may sustain frontal lobe injuries due to sports, recreation, falls, vehicle crashes, and abuse or child abuse. Researchers caution that the relationship between frontal lobe injury and violence is ambiguous and that such injuries may cause antisocial behavior more generally. Nevertheless, clinicians should assess any history of frontal lobe injury. Similarly, the consequences of concussions, particularly multiple and more severe concussions, include depression and anxiety, and in the very long term, dementia (Tator, 2013). Youths who have experienced multiple concussions may be more likely to perpetrate or be victimized by ADV because of depressed or changed mood.

Intellectual/developmental disability (IDD) is a broad term that refers to chronic impairment and causes a child to develop atypically. People with IDDs are at increased risk for experiencing abuse victimization in general (i.e., by parents, caretakers, teachers, and others; Sobsey et al, 1995). Thus, clinicians who know that clients have an IDD should assess risk for dating abuse victimization and perpetration, and conversely, clients who have been in abusive dating relationships should be screened for IDD.

The *hypothalamic-pituitary-adrenocortical (HPA) axis* is a network in the brain that responds to stress. When infants or children experience a trauma, which may include separation from a parent, witnessing violence, or experiencing abuse or neglect, their typically elevated levels of stress (and cortisol) can change how the brain functions. These children can become hypersensitive to new perceived threats to their safety or well-being and may react with an automatic "fight or flight" response when they feel threatened. Unfortunately, what some adolescents interpret as a threat can be a misperception based on prior traumatic experiences, impaired cognition (e.g., even cognition temporarily impaired by alcohol or other intoxicants), or social information–processing deficits, and they may be quick to engage in conflict or aggression even when they are not actually in danger. Discovering if clients have been exposed to traumatic stress and explaining to them the possibility that they are reacting to perceived threats may help them gain behavioral control and have better insight into their own relationship behaviors.

2.4　Comprehensive Model

Bell and Naugle (2008) combined the behavior analytic, social learning, background-situational, and social ecological models into an integrated contextual framework. Specifically, the authors posit that IPV can be influenced by distal (e.g., childhood abuse, exposure to parental violence) and proximal antecedents (e.g., negative affect), motivating factors (e.g., drug use, emotional distress), behavioral skills or lack thereof (e.g., coping skills, conflict resolution), consequences (e.g., reinforcement, punishment), verbal rules (e.g., beliefs about violence), and discriminative stimuli (e.g., situational factors, presence of a firearm). See Figure 2 for an adapted model that includes both violence perpetration and victimization, as well as additional potentially important factors (e.g., genetic makeup).

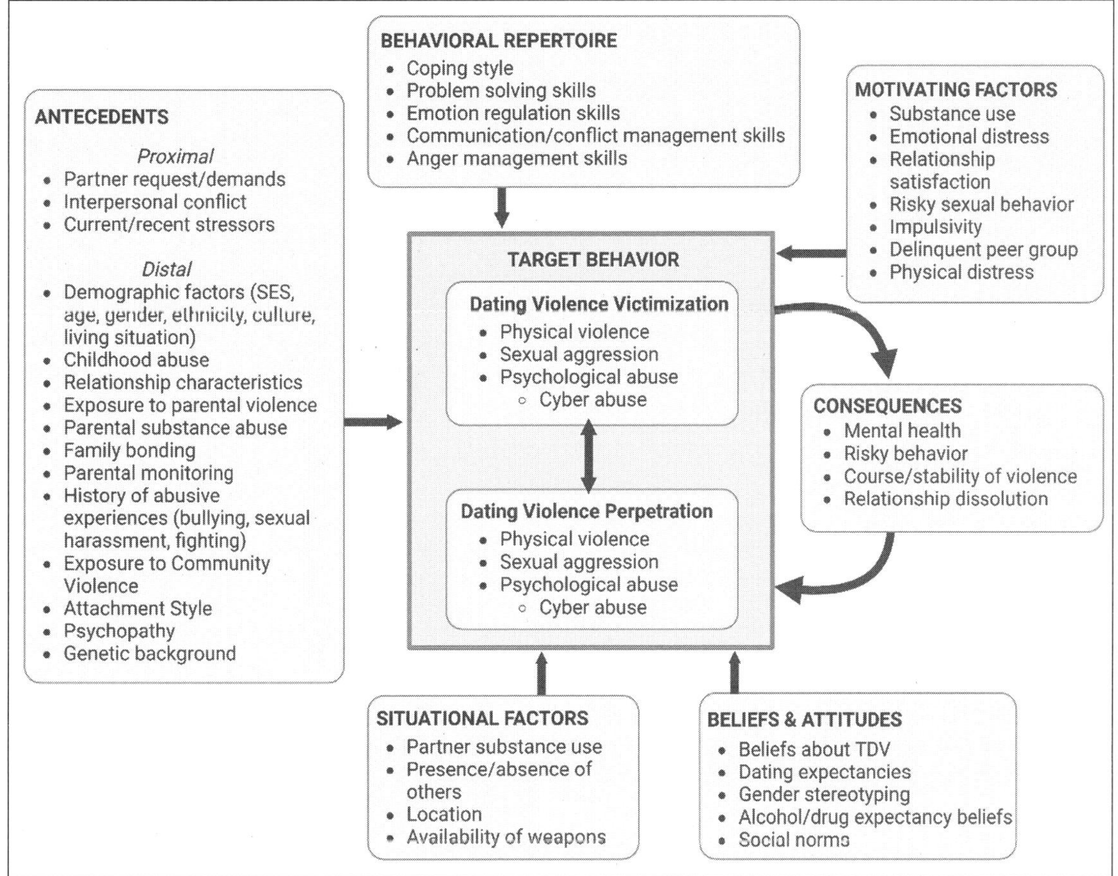

Figure 2
Conceptual framework of dating violence (adapted from Bell & Naugle, 2008, using BioRender.com). SES = socioeconomic status; TDV = teen dating violence.

Diagnosis and Treatment Indications

3.1 Differential Diagnosis and Comorbid Issues

Although the field generally agrees upon broad definitions of ADV and its subtypes (see Section 1.2), identifying and differentiating ADV from general relationship conflict or an adolescent's general emotion dysregulation in clinical treatment is less straightforward. For one, ADV is consistently and robustly linked with a host of mental health problems, both as a consequence and as a causal or maintaining factor of the psychopathology. Indeed, reviews consistently document comorbidities between ADV and depression, anxiety, substance abuse, and posttraumatic stress disorder (PTSD; see, e.g., Park et al., 2018). These difficulties have been shown to persist into adulthood, putting individuals at continued risk for depression, suicidality, substance misuse, weapons carrying and criminal behavior, and future victimization (Exner-Cortens et al., 2013; Jouriles et al., 2017; Nahapetyan et al., 2014).

Clinically, signs of ADV may be subtle, often arising in the context of other concerns. Below, we discuss: (1) general guidelines for clinicians regarding healthy dating relationships, unhealthy dating relationships, and abusive dating relationships, as well as (2) a list of commonly comorbid or related problems youths may be more readily willing to disclose in treatment. Notably, presence of an internalizing or externalizing disorder is strongly associated with subsequent involvement in physical ADV by age 21 (McCauley et al., 2015). Thus, we encourage ADV screening among all treatment-seeking youths, particularly when encountering symptom patterns outlined in this section. This recommendation is widely touted and supported in the literature, yet practical barriers to implementing wide-spread universal screening present challenges.

Dating in adolescence is often fulfilling, developmentally expected, and a necessary scaffolding for navigating future relationships. On the other hand, dating is "risky," as it introduces novel opportunities for distress (breakups, jealousy, sexual debut, relationship churning) and new social networks – specifically, other dating adolescents who may be more precocious than their nondating peers. Not every unpleasant or conflictual experience in a romantic relationship should be considered abusive, violent, or even unhealthy. On the contrary, disagreement in close relationships is unavoidable and provides opportunities to develop one's skills in constructive communication, self-reflection, perspective taking, and intimacy. Thus,

Relationship Spectrum		
Healthy Relationship	**Unhealthy Relationship**	**Abusive or Violent Relationship**
• Communication • Mutual respect • Trusting and honest • Equal decision making in choices (leisure time, finances) • Enjoy each other • Enjoy personal time (away from each other)	• Lack of communication • Disrespectful • Dishonest and not trustworthy • Unequal in decision making • Do not enjoy spending time together. • Only spending time together	• Harmful or threatening • Controlling • Violent • Preventing from seeing or contacting friends and family • Mistreating • Gaslighting

Figure 3

The relationship spectrum. Adapted from https://www.loveisrespect.org/everyone-deserves-a-healthy-relationship/relationship-spectrum/.

equipping youth with a developmentally appropriate, graded understanding of what behaviors and interactions may be healthy, unhealthy, or abusive (see Figure 3), can provide both validation for normative experiences (e.g., a difficult yet healthy breakup) and increased awareness and support for youths in unsafe partnerships.

3.1.1 Trauma- and Stressor-Related Disorders

Trauma and stressor-related disorders include exposure to a traumatic or stressful event as an explicit diagnostic criterion. Thus, PTSD, acute stress disorder, and adjustment disorders may be rooted in an ADV victimization experience. When considering PTSD and acute stress disorder in the context of ADV, bear in mind that (1) diagnosis requires that trauma exposure pre-date relevant symptoms; and (2) DSM-5-TR limits *trauma exposure* by distinct and specific guidelines to include death, serious injury, or sexual violence (APA, 2022). Although serious injury leaves room for clinical judgment, we encourage careful discernment regarding "Big T" and "little t" traumas as they relate to diagnosis, treatment, and psychiatric outcomes (Straussner & Calnan, 2014). Fortunately, most adolescents are incredibly resilient, and not all trauma exposure results in a trauma or stressor-related disorder (or other psychopathology).

In addition to trauma exposure, a diagnosis of PTSD or acute stress disorder necessitates one or more intrusion symptoms associated with the traumatic event, one or more persistent avoidance symptoms associated with the traumatic event, two or more negative alternations in cognitions and mood associated with the traumatic event, and two or more marked alterations in arousal and reactivity associated with the traumatic event, which result in clinically significant distress or impairment (APA, 2022). Of note, *complex trauma* (sometimes called *polyvictimization*) is defined as exposure to multiple traumatic events during development and may include experiences of ADV that do not necessarily individually meet DSM-5-TR criteria for PTSD

Specific acts may not result in a trauma-related disorder, but may contribute to a traumatized patient profile

(APA, 2022). Nevertheless, research is clear that repeated, prolonged, or cumulative exposure to traumatic experiences complicates healthy development and poses significant risk for psychopathology and maladjustment (Cloitre et al., 2009). Clinicians must consider both sides of the coin: Some acts of violence may not result in a trauma or stressor-related disorder, yet those small acts of violence also may meaningfully contribute to a traumatized, at-risk patient profile.

3.1.2　About Borderline Personality Disorder

Borderline personality disorder (BPD) is widely considered to be etiologically shaped by trauma, and there are high rates of co-occurrence with PTSD (Pagura et al., 2010). Late adolescents and emerging adults may present to treatment with a pervasive pattern of volatile relationships and difficulty regulating emotions. Many symptoms of BPD are risk factors associated with ADV involvement, and research links borderline features to ADV perpetration and victimization even after statistically controlling for factors such as alcohol use and exposure to parental domestic violence (Reuter et al., 2015).

BPD traits like emotional instability and impulsivity can heighten adolescents' risk for dating conflict and ADV

Specifically, BPD can include frantic efforts to avoid real or imagined abandonment, intense and volatile interpersonal relationships marked by alternating extremes of idealization and devaluation, impulsivity in potentially self-damaging areas such as risky sex and substance use, affective instability and reactive mood, inappropriately intense anger or difficulty controlling one's anger, and stress-related paranoid ideation. These experiences may put youths and emerging adults at high risk for dating partner conflict, poor emotion regulation, and difficulty maintaining healthy, violence-free romantic relationships. Although there is debate among experts about the utility or appropriateness of diagnosing BPD prior to adulthood, patterns of borderline symptoms may be useful to identify when screening for ADV or addressing maladaptive relationship behaviors in treatment.

3.1.3　Disruptive, Impulse-Control, and Conduct Disorders

ADV victimization and perpetration have been linked to generalized delinquency among adolescents (Spencer et al., 2021). Thus, youths exhibiting features of *disruptive, impulse-control,* and *conduct disorders* warrant special attention and assessment of potential ADV experiences. In contrast to other diagnostic clusters characterized by problems in emotional and behavioral regulation, these disorders involve behaviors that violate the safety and rights of others. For example, conduct disorder is characterized by a persistent pattern of behaviors that violate social norms and expectations, which can be illustrated by aggression toward people. Indeed, diagnostic indicators include threatening or intimidating others, initiating physical fights, using a weapon against others, forcing someone into sexual activity, or deliberately destroying others' property – all of which are recognized forms of ADV when perpetrated against a dating partner.

Other specific conduct disorder symptoms, such as absconding behavior (i.e., runaways), truancy, and absenteeism, are also common among youths with ADV experiences (Cheung et al., 2023). ADV perpetration can also occur in the context of aggressive outbursts seen in intermittent explosive disorder, which is marked by a failure to control impulsive aggressive behavior in response to subjectively experienced provocation.

Youths show elevated odds of ADV for each diagnosed externalizing disorder they have, and this association is stronger for females than males (McCauley et al., 2015). This may reflect a pattern whereby females with externalizing disorders are more likely to affiliate with older dating partners, which may increase risk for ADV victimization.

Substance Use Disorders

Substance (mis)use is an identified predictor *and* outcome of ADV involvement. Research consistently documents links between general substance (mis)use and ADV (see, e.g., Choi et al., 2017; Temple et al., 2013). As such, adolescents presenting to treatment with substance use concerns should be screened for ADV and other trauma exposure. Youths and young adults presenting to emergency departments for substance abuse show higher rates of ADV (22%) than their counterparts in school or community settings (around 10%), with significant associations between severity of alcohol use, younger age of drinking onset, and likelihood of ADV (Singh et al., 2015). Among those at greatest risk for future physical ADV experiences are females with substance use disorders (McCauley et al., 2015).

Substance intoxication increases the likelihood of ADV victimization and perpetration by interfering with one's inhibition, judgment and risk awareness, communication, and ability to make sober, clear-minded choices regarding personal boundaries and sexual consent. Regarding perpetration, substance use works in concert with other aggression-provoking factors to lower the threshold for violence via reduced inhibition (Reyes et al., 2015). Substance use is less likely to lead to perpetration, however, in the absence of other aggression-provoking factors. Substance use alone is not an excuse for ADV perpetration, however isolated or rare the violence may be. Working with youths to acknowledge the risks of their substance use, while simultaneously recognizing other situational and dispositional factors contributing to violence perpetration, can support productive change.

Substance use can increase ADV risk by lowering inhibition and judgment – it does not excuse or justify violence

Beyond risk, substance use may act as a self-medicating coping mechanism for posttraumatic stress and other psychiatric symptoms. Substance use may be used in attempts to dampen negative affect, enhance positive affect, and numb hyperarousal and posttraumatic stress. Particularly given the tumultuous neurocognitive developmental changes during adolescence, the immediacy of symptom relief from substance use (however short-term or maladaptive) may be attractive to teens. Finally, many other variables complicate the link between substance use and ADV. For example, teens who use drugs and alcohol may have substance-abusing caregivers or may be exposed to parental IPV or child maltreatment, and thus it becomes difficult to disentangle the effects of genetics, modeling, and abuse experiences on youths' ADV or substance use.

3.1.4 Mood Disorders, Suicidality, and Nonsuicidal Self-Harm

Depressive mood symptoms are consistent correlates of ADV involvement (see, e.g., Exner-Cortens et al., 2013). *Major depressive disorder* (MDD) is characterized by five or more of the following symptoms most of the day nearly every day across the same 2-week period: depressed mood (or irritable mood in adolescents), anhedonia, significant weight loss or weight gain outside of intentional dieting or a marked decrease or increase in appetite, observable slowing down of thoughts or physical movement, fatigue or loss of energy, feelings of worthlessness or excessive guilt, difficulties with concentration or indecisiveness, and suicidal ideation. At least one of the five symptoms must be low mood or anhedonia (APA, 2022).

As is always the case when screening for mood disorders, it is imperative to assess any history of hypomanic or manic episodes. A history of *bipolar I or II* diagnosis has been linked to later ADV (McCauley et al., 2015). One explanation for this link is that bipolar mood features may put youths at heightened risk for ADV involvement via symptoms of general difficulties in emotion regulation (particularly during periods of irritable or expansive mood), increased impulsivity, risky sexual or substance use behaviors, or delusional thinking.

Disruptive mood dysregulation disorder (DMDD), akin to behaviors exhibited in the disruptive, impulse-control, and conduct disorders, can include verbal rages and physical aggression toward others. In DMDD, aggression is grossly out of proportion in intensity or duration, to the situation or provocation, and occurs in multiple settings. These outbursts must occur, on average, three or more times weekly, and mood between outbursts is consistently and markedly irritable or angry to the extent that it is observable by others (APA, 2022).

The link between suicidality and ADV is well-documented (Baiden et al., 2021; Nahapetyan et al., 2014). Further, depressive symptoms appear to mediate, or explain, some of this connection (Kim et al., 2018). Thus, youths with a clearly differentiated mood disorder diagnosis or other psychiatric comorbidity that "explains" symptoms of suicidal ideation, nevertheless warrant screening for trauma exposure, including ADV. *Nonsuicidal self-injury* (NSSI) is conceptualized as repeated self-injury inflicted to reduce negative affect or resolve interpersonal difficulty. Common methods of injury are cutting skin with a knife, needle, razor, or other sharp objects in areas such as the thighs or forearms with superficial cuts. Onset of NSSI often occurs in early adolescence. Accumulating evidence links NSSI and ADV, although further research is warranted (Hatkevich et al., 2020; Rizzo et al., 2014).

3.1.5 Anxiety Disorders

Due to the variety of anxiety symptoms and disorders associated with ADV, we recommend that clinicians assess for all anxiety disorders when evaluating an individual presenting with ADV. One anxiety disorder relatively common among adolescents and emerging adults, *generalized anxiety disorder* (GAD), is characterized by excessive worry or anxious thoughts that are difficult to manage. These symptoms may be theoretically related to increased uncertainty regarding the onset, severity, or frequency of abuse in one's romantic relationships, or ambiguous cues from one's dating partner that "clue them in" to potential ADV occurrence. Beyond cognitive elements of GAD, behavioral and somatic symptoms are also involved, such as fatigue, impaired sleep, and muscle tension. Affective symptoms of GAD may include irritability.

3.1.6 Other Comorbidities

In addition to psychiatric diagnostic clusters, numerous research studies have documented that ADV often co-occurs with other physical and psychosocial concerns, including, but not limited to, ADV-related physical injury (e.g., bruising, lacerations, traumatic brain injury, or broken bones) as well as comorbid trauma victimization and perpetration (e.g., peer violence or bullying, child maltreatment, adolescent domestic battery, or exposure to domestic violence).

3.2 Diagnostic Procedures and Documentation

There are no DSM-5-TR or *International Classification of Diseases* (ICD) codes specific to ADV victimization or perpetration. However, DSM-5-TR includes codes for adult spouse or partner violence of physical, psychological, and sexual subtypes, with codes for meetings with victims and perpetrators (see codes with stem 995.8; APA, 2022). If there is no active diagnosis of spouse or partner abuse, but historically this type of abuse was present, V codes are used. These include V15.41 or V61.11 for victim counseling (including physical, sexual, and psychological abuse), V61.11 for psychological abuse victim counseling, and V61.12 for perpetrator counseling. The relevant *International Classification of Diseases*, 11th revision (ICD-11) code is QE51.0: relationship distress with spouse or partner, which can be further coded as history of violence (QE51.1), other specified problem associated with interactions with spouse or partner (QE51.Y), or unspecified problems (QE51.Z) (World Health Organization [WHO], 2022). Although some forms of child maltreatment as listed in DSM-5-TR may appear to apply to adolescent victims of dating violence under age 18, these codes are not used, as child maltreatment is specifically defined by DSM-5-TR as abuse perpetrated by a caregiver (APA, 2022).

As such, adolescents receiving treatment for experiences of ADV are often diagnosed or otherwise coded for treatment under comorbid issues, such as an Unspecified Trauma- and Stressor-Related Disorder 309.9, among others. The lack of a specific DSM-5-TR or ICD code for ADV has a few consequences. Formal documentation of youths identified as involved in ADV during emergency care (e.g., emergency room or psychiatric hospitalization) or through broad universal screenings (e.g., school health clinic) becomes limited or absent.

Furthermore, ADV victimization and perpetration are not readily identifiable in chart review across practitioners or settings, potentially limiting the effectiveness of individual treatment. Case conceptualization would benefit from such documentation that may elucidate patterns of interpersonal dysfunction. Moreover, the absence of formal documentation contributes to outdated ideas that diminish the severity and impact of ADV. In contrast, outside of medical professions, ADV perpetration can result in formal legal charges such as aggravated assault, stalking, and sexual assault, among others. Taken together, we see a double bind: ADV victimization is not reified with a psychiatric code for youths, while ADV perpetration can be used to punish, stigmatize, and incarcerate juveniles.

Again, signs of ADV may be subtle, ambiguous, and resistantly endorsed by youths. We recommend screening early, often, and sensitively to detect violent dating experiences among adolescents. This approach, although tedious at times, promotes youth safety and errs on the side of picking up false positives over potentially missing a true instance of abuse.

Recognizing, reporting, and disclosing ADV in clinical practice is rarely straightforward, requiring clinical sensitivity and careful consideration. States and facilities may vary in legal or procedural standards for reporting violence among adolescents, particularly those adolescents yet to reach the age of majority or consent. All states, the District of Columbia, the Commonwealth of Puerto Rico, and several US territories have statutes identifying persons who are required to report child maltreatment under specific circumstances. Relevant to ADV, this may include reporting of children at risk of imminent danger (e.g., a runaway or homeless youth under age 18 residing with their perpetrator).

In detention settings, clinicians must balance mandated reporting, youth safety, and therapeutic trust

Similarly, practitioners working with youths and emerging adults within detention or incarceration facilities may encounter exceptions to clinical confidentiality when reports of ADV impact the safety of that youth or others in the facility and/or take place in the context of court-mandated treatment. Ethically balancing legal requirements (e.g., mandated reporting), youth safety, and the clinical utility of breaking confidentiality (i.e., avoiding or accelerating ruptures in therapeutic alliance) is complex. The benefits of professional consultation and supervision, where appropriate, cannot be overstated in these circumstances.

3.3   Assessment

No single measure is considered the gold standard for ADV identification and assessment; thus, professional best practice should be utilized whenever possible (Table 2). This includes use of multiple data sources (i.e., self-report, caregiver report, clinical interview, behavioral observations, and/or records review) and continued monitoring throughout treatment, with reevaluation conducted as necessary. Below we introduce both behaviorally based (i.e., act frequencies) measures of ADV as well as attitudinal indicators of ADV risk or involvement.

Despite diagnostic limitations, advances in interpersonal violence research offer helpful measurement tools for assessing the frequency, duration, and extent of ADV violence. Measurement is often selected based on researcher or clinician goals. Many professionals rely on behaviorally based measures of ADV, such that respondents provide frequencies for specific violent acts (experienced as either victim or perpetrator). Advantages to this approach include specificity of the act experienced, as well as getting around youth (mis)perceptions regarding sexual assault or appropriate dating behavior (e.g., items that assess "They kissed me when I didn't want them to" vs. "I was sexually assaulted"). Selecting developmentally appropriate behavioral assessments is paramount – the reading level, sexual maturity, and experiences relevant to a 21-year-old are unlikely to be the same as those of an 11-year-old navigating early puberty.

Attitude-driven measures are also commonly used, particularly among researchers. These assessments tap adolescents' attitudes around the acceptability of interpersonal aggression, belief in harmful stereotypes (e.g., rape myths), and agreement with imbalanced or violent power dynamics.

Table 2
Commonly Used ADV Measures

Measure	Citation	Construct assessed
Behavior, acts, and frequencies		
1. Conflict in Adolescent Dating Relationships Inventory (CADRI)	Wolfe et al. (2001)	Frequency of victimization and perpetration in past 12 months. Covers subtypes of physical violence, verbal abuse, threatening behavior, sexual violence, relational aggression, and positive conflict resolution skills.
2. Measure of Adolescent Relationship Harassment and Abuse (see Appendix)	Rothman, Paruk, et al. (2022)	Dating partner perpetration of social media control, stalking, physical, emotional, and sexual violence, and intimidation.
3. Youth Risk Behavior Survey (YRBS)	Mpofu et al. (2023)	Victimization in past 12 months.
4. Revised Conflict Tactic Scales (CTS-2)	Straus et al. (1996)	Frequency of negotiation, psychological aggression, physical assault, sexual coercion, and injury victimization, and perpetration.

Table 2   Continued

Measure	Citation	Construct assessed
5. Lifetime Trauma and Victimization History – Youth Version (LTVH)	Widom et al. (2005)	Victimization (physical and sexual), including age of incident.
6. Safe Dates Scale	Foshee et al. (1996)	Frequency of physical and sexual victimization and perpetration.
Attitudes		
7. Attitude About Aggression in Dating Situations (AADS)	Slep et al. (2001)	Agreement with aggressive behavior male-to-female, female-to-male, and same-sex peers within dating context (physical aggression shown previously as provoking aggressive responses).
8. Justification Verbal/ Coercive Tactics Scale (JVCT)	Slep et al. (2001)	Attitudes about the justifiability of verbal aggression, controlling behaviors, and jealous behaviors directed toward males or females within a dating relationship (emotionally aggressive behaviors that may be more normative than physical aggression).
9. Illinois Rape Myth Acceptance Scale (IRMA)	Payne et al. (1999)	Five items to measure rape myth acceptance on a 5-point Likert scale (male-to-female violence).
10. Attitudes Towards Male/ Female Dating Violence (AMDV; AFDV)	Price et al. (1999)	Attitudes about heterosexual physical, psychological and sexual dating violence among adolescents of all ages.
11. Adolescent Attitudes Regarding Dating Relationships (AARDR)	Davidson (2005)	Attitudes in high school students toward dating violence and healthy dating relationships. One measure for males' attitudes and one for females' attitudes.
12. Normative Beliefs About Aggression scale (NOBAGS)	Huesmann & Guerra (1997)	Approval of aggression in young and older children.

Note. ADV = adolescent dating violence

3.3.1   Clinical Interviewing for ADV

In addition to data derived from the measures listed in Table 2, clinical interview is necessary to develop a comprehensive picture of the adolescent's dating experiences. Clinicians should approach the clinical interview with the same thoughtfulness, sensitivity, and open-ended questioning used to assess other mental health concerns. As a basic guide, in Box 1 are suggestions of elements to include when conducting a clinical interview relevant to ADV:

> **Box 1**
> **Elements of ADV Clinical Interview**
>
> **Dating experiences**
> - Age of first dating experiences, age of sexual debut, current relationship status
> - History of dating partners (number of partners, gender of partners, length of relationship)
> - Context of relationships as labeled by youth (e.g., "friends with benefits," long-term dating partner, polyamorous, monogamous, etc.)
> - Onset, frequency, and duration of ADV in each relationship reported
>   - Youth's experience as victim and/or perpetrator
>   - Presence and extent of injuries and if medical care was sought
>   - Youth's perception of why or how violence unfolded
>   - Follow-up questions at provider's discretion around any acts or attitudes reported on self-report scales
>
> **Psychiatric and physical health history**
> - History of head trauma, major illness/injury, pregnancy
> - History of other interpersonal trauma (e.g., child maltreatment)
> - Developmental screen (e.g., prenatal exposure to IPV, presence of IDD)
> - Other general psychodiagnostic assessment (e.g., mood disorders, anxiety disorders, suicidality, substance use, etc.)
>
> **Safety**
> - Imminent safety risks to self, other, or by ADV victimization
> - Preparations, if any, for safe exit from relationships if needed
> - Awareness and use of safe sexual practices

3.3.2 Violence Risk Assessments

Depending on treatment setting, referring agency, and treatment goals, a formal forensic risk assessment may be necessary and beneficial. Risk assessments utilize clinical interviews and data sources to estimate the probability or likelihood of future dangerousness, harm, or recidivism. Cases where this may be appropriate include justice-involved individuals receiving court-mandated rehabilitation following a sexual offense or domestic violence charge.

Importantly, research has yet to identify any single best or error-free risk assessment. As a result, this information should be viewed as a small part of a more comprehensive examination of an individual's risk and protective factors.

The Risk and Needs Assessment Guide, Juvenile Sex Offender Assessment Protocol – II (J-SOAP-II; Prentky & Righthand, 2003) is a structured professional judgment guide used to systematically examine the presence and extent of four factors associated with increased risk for reoffending among youths who have committed sexual offenses. This assessment tool incorporates both static and dynamic risk factors. The former are those that are not likely to change over time and thus will likely continue to pose risk throughout development (such as age of offense, offense type, offense history, and other historical factors).

Dynamic risk factors are those that can change with proper interventions (such as thinking patterns, living situation, and social skills). The first domain includes history of atypical or deviant sexual interests and behaviors and/or sexual preoccupation or hypersexual behaviors. The second domain examined involves the youth's historical tendency to behave impulsively and to engage in antisocial behaviors. The third factor examined involves a juvenile's level of responsibility for sexual offenses, expression of genuine remorse and empathy, and motivation to avoid future offending. The fourth domain examined involves the youth's recent behaviors in the community, as well as level of community and family support.

The Protective + Risk Observations for Eliminating Sexual Offense Recidivism (PROFESOR; Worling, 2017) is a structured checklist designed to summarize protective and risk factors of adolescents with sexual offenses. Specifically, this tool contains 20 factors assessing protective and risk characteristics on bipolar indices and is intended to inform intervention planning to reduce sexual recidivism.

The Structured Assessment of Violence Risk in Youth (SAVRY; Meyers & Schmidt, 2008) is a structured professional judgment tool that focuses on relevant risk factors derived from research and professional literature on adolescent development and violence. This tool uses 24 items covering three risk domains rated on a 3-point scale (low, moderate, or high), including historical risk factors, social/contextual risk factors, and individual/clinical factors. The SAVRY also addresses six protective factors, marked present or absent.

3.3.3 · Related Measures Relevant to ADV Treatment

Although not specific to ADV, the following constructs and example assessment instruments may prove fruitful in conceptualizing and monitoring treatment progress when ADV is of therapeutic concern. In addition to specific instruments listed in this section, resources such as The National Child Traumatic Stress Network (https://nctsn.org) offer searchable measure reviews for clinicians and researchers to select and access appropriate assessment tools.

Posttraumatic Stress Symptoms

Commonly used well-validated assessments of posttraumatic stress among adolescents include the *Clinician-Administered PTSD Scale for DSM-5 – Child/Adolescent Version* (CAPS-CA-5; Pynoos et al., 2015), the *UCLA Child/Adolescent PTSD Reaction Index for DSM-5* (Kaplow et al., 2020), and the *Trauma Symptom Checklist for Children* (TSCC; Briere, 1996). The CAPS-CA-5 comprises clinician-administered items derived from the DSM-5 symptom criteria for PTSD as defined for youths 7 years or older. This assessment is based on an original CAPS-5 assessment, with modifications to include picture responses and age-appropriate items. Items include standardized prompts and follow-up questions to accurately assess the onset and duration of symptoms, subjective distress, perceived functional and developmental impact of symptoms, and dissociation subtype (depersonalization, derealization). Additionally, the measure is intended to probe global symptom severity, overall response validity, and improvement (if any) in symptoms since a previous assessment administration.

The UCLA Child/Adolescent PTSD Reaction Index for DSM-5-TR is a semistructured interview of trauma history and PTSD symptoms among school-age children and adolescents. The TSCC is a 54-item scale appropriate for youths aged 8 to 16 years to assess posttraumatic stress symptoms. Subscales cover anxiety, depression, anger, posttraumatic stress, dissociation, and sexual concerns. Eight critical items flag clinical issues of imminent importance, such as homicidal or suicidal urges.

Emotion Regulation

The *Difficulties in Emotion Regulation Scale Short Form* (DERS-SF; Kaufman et al., 2016) can be used to assess four dimensions of emotional regulation among adolescents and adults. Six subscales are included: nonacceptance of emotional responses, difficulty engaging in goal-directed behavior (when experiencing negative affect), impulse control difficulties, lack of emotional awareness, limited access to emotion regulation strategies, and lack of emotional clarity.

Anger Expression

The *State-Trait Anger Expression Inventory–2* has versions for both young adult and adolescent use (STAXI-2; Spielberger, 1999). This tool is a 35-item self-report of state and trait anger expression and control. The Child-Adolescent version can be administered to youths aged 9–18 years.

Hostile Attributions and Violent Cognitions

The *Firestone Assessment of Violent Thoughts, Adolescent Version* (FAVT-A; Firestone & Firestone, 2008) is a self-report measure aimed at assessing thoughts that predispose violence. The tool includes measures for thoughts related to paranoia or suspiciousness, persecutory ideations, self-deprecation, and overt aggression.

4

Treatment

We have now reviewed the prevalence of ADV, descriptive epidemiology, and theoretical explanations for its causation. The theoretical explanations included factors pertaining to individuals' neuropsychology and biology, psychological traits, experiences in childhood and with peers, and neighborhood and societal and structural factors. The next important question to answer is, how should perpetrators and victims of ADV be treated, and which treatment approaches are effective?

To answer that question, we will need to define what it means for a treatment to "work," the various options for treatment and support, the range of evidence that has been used to support these options, therapist skills for engaging with youths who have been in abusive relationships, and issues relating to culture, the criminal justice system, and the mental health service provision system that can influence how and whether youths receive treatment.

4.1   Envisioning Successful Outcomes for Treatment of ADV

When most people think about whether a treatment for violent aggression is successful, we suspect that they want to know the chances that participating in treatment will "cure" somebody of violent impulses entirely – and how reasonable it is to expect the individual will never again engage in violence. While this is one definition of success, it is at the very far end of a spectrum of what might count as successful outcomes for treatment. It is unrealistic to expect any one treatment, or even a combination of treatments, to permanently eradicate all aggressive behavior.

Similarly, when it comes to survivors of ADV, it is perhaps unreasonable to expect any one type of supportive service or treatment to ensure that the patient will be in perfectly healthy relationships from then on. By way of comparison, we tend not to hold other types of treatments to the same high standard. For example, most people who are suffering from a cough and take a cough suppressant medicine do not expect that the medicine will stop them from coughing even once ever again. While most people may generally accept that not all pharmaceutical treatments are 100% effective for all people, it does appear to be difficult for many to endorse any treatment for

ADV as effective because only a minority of participants may benefit and for a short duration.

Another reason it is difficult to provide a lengthy list of treatment modalities and options that are known to be effective for treating dating abuse is that – unlike some other conditions, such as depression, anxiety, or attention-deficit/hyperactivity disorder (ADHD) – comparatively few resources have been devoted to developing and testing ADV treatments. ADV was not a topic of research investigation until the late 1980s–1990s, and the early studies were primarily focused on establishing prevalence, incidence, and descriptive information about which youths were most at risk. The idea that treatments should be evaluated for effect did not come into favor until the early 2000s, and then researchers faced competition for limited funding. What is more, when funding was available, emphasis was placed on discovering effective prevention strategies to stop ADV before it ever started in the first place, rather than treatments that would support survivors or change the behavior of perpetrators.

A final reason it has historically been difficult to determine effective treatments is that some interventions may be effective at reducing psychological ADV perpetration, but not physical or sexual perpetration (Rothman et al., 2020), while others may be effective at reducing physical, but not sexual, abuse.

Research on the treatment of ADV is limited, historically focused on prevention, and effectiveness varies by abuse type

4.2   Methods of Treatment

Given the scope and impact of ADV, there is a clear need for effective intervention and prevention efforts. Results of a recent meta-analysis support the overall efficacy of existing programs on reducing TDV perpetration and victimization (Russell et al., 2021). Yet only 25% of US adolescents report exposure to an ADV prevention or intervention program in the past year (Finkelhor et al., 2014). This is regrettable, especially given the sizeable and growing research literature of empirically supported programs.

Systematic literature reviews have identified over 60 unique programs specifically developed and tested to address ADV (see, e.g., De La Rue et al., 2017). These programs vary in several ways, from the intended population (e.g., perpetrator-focused, victim-focused, bystander-focused), to the setting (e.g., classroom, juvenile justice, community outpatient facilities), to attitudinal and behavioral treatment targets (e.g., rape myths, bystander behaviors, perpetration rates), to delivery methods (e.g., small group discussions, one-on-one therapy, parent–child group sessions).

Although individual existing programs may conceptualize ADV slightly differently, draw from various theories, or tackle diverse determinants, a common underlying assumption is that violence is a public health problem. The public health approach prioritizes population-level violence reduction to maximize benefits to the largest number of people (Figure 4). This necessitates strong data on the incidence, prevalence, and course of ADV

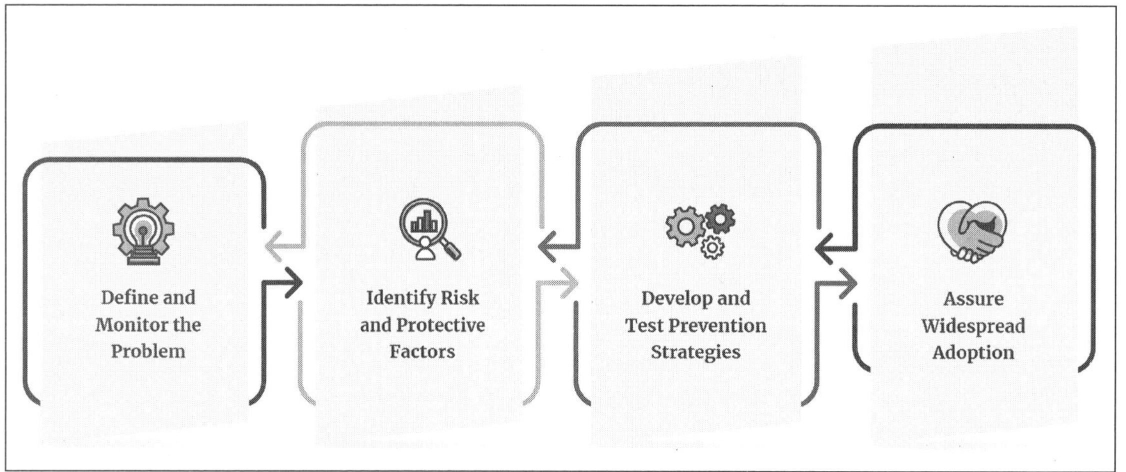

Figure 4
The public health approach to violence prevention. Reproduced from US Centers for Disease Control and Prevention, 2024. (Use of this material does not constitute endorsement of the authors by the US Government, Department of Health and Human Services, or Centers for Disease Control and Prevention.)

(i.e., defining and monitoring the problem), ongoing research on static and dynamic risk and protective factors, empirically supported prevention strategies, and efforts to promote widespread adoption of evidence-based violence reduction practices.

Implementation components include factors such as participant characteristics, prevention approach, presenter, setting, length, and format – that is, the *Who, What, Where, When,* and *How* of delivering an intervention. Below we provide example programs for each implementation component. This list is nonexhaustive, reflecting some of the empirically tested and theory-driven programs available today. In looking at the organization of these interventions, note that subheadings are not mutually exclusive – for example, we describe the *Fourth R* as being within group-based programs (*How*), whereas that also fits under subheadings of school-based programs (*Where*) and is an example of primary prevention (*What*).

4.2.1   ADV Prevention Implementation: Who

Participant characteristics (i.e., *Who*) can include demographic data, such as participant sex and racial or ethnic makeup of intended audience, that ultimately contribute to culturally relevant differences in programming. Trends in program evaluation research reveal most tested interventions are coeducational (i.e., delivered to both male and female youths) and presented with majority White youths in mind. Below we outline exceptions to these trends, providing examples of single-sex and culturally specific options.

Examples of Gender-Based (i.e., Single-Sex) Programs

Coaching Boys Into Men (Miller et al., 2012) is a comprehensive curriculum designed to equip athletic coaches with tools to reduce acceptance and perpetration of violence against women and girls by young male athletes. This program is theorized to modify norms that foster and exacerbate gender-based violence, by equipping male athletic coaches as prosocial role models. Coaches guide athletes through weekly 15-minute discussions for 11 weeks. The program is gender-specific, so materials are geared toward strategies, scenarios, and resources needed to talk to boys about healthy relationships, ADV, sexual assault, and gender-based harassment.

The intervention components of Coaching Boys Into Men include (1) raising awareness (coaches define healthy and unhealthy dating behaviors), (2) promoting gender-equitable attitudes and norms (coaches promote healthy masculinity and male sexuality); and (3) bystander intervention (coaches model bystander intervention skills). Miller and colleagues (2012) hypothesize that these components result in decreased ADV perpetration and increased bystander intervention via increased awareness of abuse, increased positive gender-equitable attitudes, and increased intentions to intervene as bystanders with peers. Specifically, they found that athletes receiving the intervention, relative to their counterparts in the control condition, had a higher likelihood of intervening, reported higher levels of positive bystander intervention behavior. Counter to expectations, they did not identify changes in gender-equitable attitudes, recognition of abusive behaviors, DV perpetration.

Whereas Coaching Boys Into Men and similar programs are designed to reduce perpetration of gender-based violence by adolescent males, *My Voice, My Choice* (Rowe et al., 2015) is structured to reduce ADV victimization by empowering adolescent females to set psychologically and physically safe boundaries. My Voice, My Choice provides psychoeducation and skills rehearsal around assertive resistance as a form of self-protection from unwanted sexual advances. Assertive resistance is characterized by confident, firm, and unwavering refusal that escalates to meet the dangerousness of the situation or perpetrator.

This program is unique in its use of virtual reality to walk participants through realistic, immersive role-play opportunities to practice their assertive resistance skills during a single 90-minute group session. Sessions include discussion, modeling of assertive resistance skills, virtual reality practice, and facilitator feedback.

Examples of Culture-Specific Programs

Gonzalez-Guarda and colleagues (2015) developed and tested a program specifically designed for Latino and Hispanic youth called *JOVEN/YOUTH: Juntos Opuestos a la Violence Entre Novios/Together Against Dating Violence*. This program is currently manualized in both English and Spanish and was developed with input from adolescent focus groups, a community domestic violence agency, local public school, and university research personnel. The program draws from ecodevelopmental and social cognitive theories.

JOVEN consists of six large group sessions, two sessions for parents, and two for school staff (Table 3). Sessions include psychoeducation and skill-building activities administered via videos, music, phone photography, group discussion, and role-plays. In the final session, parents practice healthy negotiation skills around curfews and dating, directly with their teen.

Table 3
Overview of JOVEN

Participants	Session title	Topics
Adolescents	Hispanic traditions, pop culture, and dating	Gender and relationship norms; Hispanic cultural influences; generational changes; dating in era of social media; the role of media in influencing norms
	Healthy and unhealthy relationships in Hispanic culture	ADV in Hispanic adolescents; characteristics of unhealthy and healthy relationships; teen power and control wheel; respectful behaviors; warning signs
	Sex and drugs	Adolescent sexual development; normative risky sexual substance abuse behaviors in Hispanic culture; safe and safer sexual practices
	Legal rights and accessing services	Laws relating to immigration, dating and domestic violence and sexual health; school policies; the role of police; community services; safety planning
	Life and bystander skills	Conflict management skills; handling breakups in relationships; skills to avoid risky situations and peer pressure; prosocial behaviors in Hispanic families
	Speaking up	Assertive communication; positive communication strategies; applications to communication with girlfriend/boyfriend, peers, school personnel, and parents according to culturally appropriate ways
Parents and school personnel	ADV among Hispanic youths	ADV statistics in Hispanic adolescents; power and control; warning signs; legal rights; safety planning; community resources
Parents	Effective parenting and communication practices	Parental monitoring behaviors in Hispanic families; communicating effectively with your children and their friends; prosocial behaviors relating to ADV and other risky situations; understanding and working with the school system
School personnel	Mentoring youth on relationships	Modeling healthy relationships; prosocial behaviors relating to relationships; communicating with at-risk youth; prosocial behaviors relating to ADV and other risky situations; working with parents in culturally appropriate ways

Note. ADV = adolescent dating violence; JOVEN = JOVEN/YOUTH: Juntos Opuestos a la Violence Entre Novios/Together Against Dating Violence. Reproduced with permission from Gonzalez-Guarda et al., 2015, p. 414.

Respect (Baker et al., 2014) was created for youths of Asian and Pacific Islander descent in Hawai'i. The curriculum was developed in a collaboration between a statewide abuse social services agency (Hawai'i Department of Education) and community service providers (e.g., teachers, counselors). Respect includes six classroom-based lesson plans and associated student worksheets that cover the following concepts: defining sexual violence; identifying types of sexual violence (including sexual harassment, exposure, sexual touching, and penetrative assault); defining, communicating, and respecting personal boundaries; enacting effective bystander responses to risky situations; and supporting victimized peers. Importantly, all lesson plans meet the Hawai'i Department of Education standards for health education.

Throughout the Respect curriculum, character names and references reflect Hawai'ian and broader Pacific Islander traditions. Culturally, video components of the intervention depict victim stories specifically scripted to reflect cultural subgroups of Hawai'ians portrayed by local actors. Moreover, the curriculum includes clear discussion of extended family as sources of support and cultural shame sometimes surrounding help seeking among Asian and Pacific Islander families.

Another program focusing on Latino emerging adults, *Dating Relationships Involving Violence End Now* (DRIVEN; Terrazas-Carrillo et al., 2021), is guided by social learning theory, and targets the cultural concepts of acculturation, machismo, and marianismo. *Machismo* has been linked to more tolerant attitudes of, and a higher risk for, partner violence, and *marianismo*, or being feminine, modest, and subservient to your partner, may also be a risk factor for partner violence.

4.2.2   ADV Prevention Implementation: What

Participant characteristics can also reflect program approach. Program approaches (the *What*) can include universal or primary prevention designed to affect all adolescents, selected or secondary (geared toward a subset of the population at risk), or indicated or tertiary interventions that target teens already experiencing ADV. The terms "primary," "secondary," and "tertiary" prevention are often used interchangeably with "universal," "selected," and "indicated," respectively, though these models differ slightly. A public health approach to violence prevention supports the notion that all forms of prevention – primary, secondary, and tertiary – are necessary and complementary to reduce the incidence, prevalence, and adverse impact of ADV.

Research sometimes examines only prevention approach *or* setting, potentially conflating the effects of each implementation component (i.e., to what extent efficacy is related to primary approach, school-based delivery, or both). Disentangling delivery setting from program approach affords a richer understanding of how existing programs are intended to function, and may clarify conclusions regarding best practices for reaching intended audiences.

> **Prevention programs vary by whether they are universal, selected, or indicated – all levels are needed to reduce ADV**

Primary Prevention

In line with the public health method to ADV prevention, primary prevention approaches seek to stop violence before it starts, to reduce the incidence of ADV. As such, common applications of primary prevention include universal prevention for all youths early prior to the initiation of dating in hopes of preventing ADV from ever occurring. Examples include universal school-based prevention programs and bystander interventions.

Table 4
Classroom-Based *Shifting Boundaries* Lesson Overview

Lesson	Objectives
What is a boundary?	To define boundaries – from personal through geopolitical: to define the meaning and role of boundaries in student relationships and experiences, and to introduce boundaries as a theme in literature and social studies.
Measuring personal space	To continue experiential learning and discussion of boundaries from previous lesson.
Big deal or no big deal?	To help students differentiate between behaviors that are acceptable and behaviors that are against school policy or against the law.
DVD segment on Shantai from *Flirting or Hurting* by PBS	To continue discussion and application of acceptable and unacceptable behaviors from previous lesson. Note: For the combined campus-based and classroom-based intervention, this lesson also (1) introduces students to the respecting boundaries agreements (i.e., restraining orders) in their school and (2) makes students familiar with such agreements by completing one as practice.
"Says Who" questionnaire on myths/facts about sexual harassment; "What Can I Do?" tips on possible response to being sexually harassed	To define sexual harassment; to dispel common myths about sexual harassment; to raise awareness of the prevalence of sexual harassment.
Mapping Safe and Unsafe Spaces at School	To identify where (exact locations) in the school the students feel "hot" and where they feel "cool"; (B) to help students identify these places; to provide information for the school to use in order to develop a "cooler" school environment; to empower students to transform "hot" areas into "cool" areas by examining why they consider particular locations to be "hot" and what the school can do to make those areas "cooler." *Note that campus-based intervention is limited solely to this component

Note. Based on Taylor et al., 2011. The authors gratefully acknowledge the US Department of Justice, Office of Justice Programs for allowing us to reproduce, in part or in whole, the Shifting Boundaries lesson. The opinions, findings, and conclusions or recommendations expressed in this publication are those of the authors and do not necessarily represent the official position or policies of the US Department of Justice.

Taylor and colleagues developed *Shifting Boundaries* (Taylor et al., 2011), a group of school-based interventions including classroom lessons and building-based interventions (Table 4). Classroom lessons emphasized legal definitions and consequences of ADV perpetration, federal laws around ADV and sexual harassment, communicating boundaries in interpersonal relationships, and how bystanders can prosocially interfere in situations of ADV. Lessons are generally taught over 6 to 10 weeks depending on school scheduling. Materials are covered via worksheets, quizzes, experiential activities, discussion, and applied practice.

Building-based intervention components include revising school protocols to identify and respond to ADV, introducing temporary school-based restraining orders, and poster campaigns to increase awareness and reporting of ADV to appropriate school resources. Additionally, Shifting Boundaries helps students work with school administration to locate unsafe areas of the school using hotspot mapping. Analysis of student identified hotspots considers the extent of surveillance and adult presence across areas, age of students typically congregating across areas, and looking for trends in the reasons students rated areas as more or less safe than others. Specific recommendations for responding to areas identified as dangerous (i.e., "hot") include:

- Increase the presence of school safety personnel in "hot" areas
- Put up signs in "hot" locations reminding students of their rights
- Ask the teacher whose class is nearest to a specific "hot spot" to monitor the area between class periods
- Have custodians check the lighting in "hot spots"
- Consider ways to reroute school traffic
- Designate certain areas as limited to a particular class grade (e.g. a "sixth grade–only hall")
- Send students to the restroom in pairs
- Ask a staff member to check bathrooms periodically (e.g., every 10 minutes)
- Institute a system of bathroom passes or bathroom locks

About Bystander Programs

The premise of bystander training programs is to educate all members of a community (e.g., an entire school campus) on effective bystander behaviors. Bystanders are conceptualized as witnesses or third parties to situations that pose risk for ADV or in which ADV has already occurred. Examples of effective bystander behavior include stopping a friend who is attempting to hook up with an intoxicated dating partner, expressing concern to a peer about suspected violence in their relationship, and confronting someone who is excusing abusive behavior.

Meta-analysis of college bystander programs has demonstrated moderate effects on self-efficacy for bystander behavior and small effects on actual bystander behaviors (Jouriles et al., 2018). Examples of bystander training programs for ADV include *TakeCARE* and *Green Dot* (Coker et al., 2020), both of which have been adapted for high school and college-aged youths. Note that Green Dot is reviewed in Section 4.2.4.

TakeCARE (Jouriles et al., 2016; Sargent et al., 2017) is a brief 24-minute video program that can be shown in group or individual settings, thus boasting low costs, easy implementation, and guaranteed treatment fidelity. The video begins by validating the demanding experience of high school or college students, marked by balancing increasing adult responsibilities, social opportunities, and changing peer relationships. *TakeCARE* provides information on the likelihood of ADV among friends, and how individuals can help "take care" of their friends to prevent ADV. Three vignettes illustrate and discuss effective bystander intervention and consequences of inaction in response to risky ADV situations.

Effective bystander responses are defined as behaviors that either (1) prevent the event, (2) stop it from continuing or escalating, or (3) provide support for a friend after an event takes place. In each vignette, the narrator offers several effective bystander interventions for the scenario, emphasizing that "it's not so important what you do, just that you do *something*" to protect your friends. The acronym CARE is used throughout the program to link the principles of successful bystander behavior: Effective bystanders are "C" – *confident* that they can help their friends avoid risky situations; "A" – *aware* that their friends could get hurt in these kinds of situations, "R" – *responsible* for helping; and "E" – *effective* in how they help. The video also provides definitions of ADV, coercion, and ongoing sexual consent.

Secondary

The goal of secondary prevention is to reduce the prevalence of ADV, often through early detection and intervention among youths identified as at elevated risk. An example of secondary prevention can include screening youths for ADV who present at emergency departments for injury or mental health concerns, or providing specific interventions for youths known to be at higher risk of ADV. Below we outline a few example interventions designed and tested for efficacy with groups at heightened risk for ADV involvement. Specifically, these programs target and address increased risk due to exposure to IPV, exposure to school or community violence, foster care involvement, and risky substance use.

Young pregnant women are at elevated risk of ADV involvement. In response to this high-needs population, Langhinrichsen-Rohling & Turner developed *Building a Lasting Love* (BALL; Langhinrichsen-Rohling & Turner, 2012), rooted in social learning theory and designed to improve relationship functioning among pregnant teenage adolescents and their baby's father, improve communication, enhance healthy conflict management skills, and increase adaptive emotion regulation. BALL includes four 90-minute sessions offered once weekly, with each session designed to function independently (i.e., absence at one session would not interfere with subsequent sessions). Sessions include didactic teaching, group discussion, and activities. The first session outlines healthy versus unhealthy romantic relationships, making a safety plan, and goal setting. Session 2 covers coping with negative affect in relationships, such as dealing with disrespect, managing disappointment and anger, and emotion regulation using nonviolent strategies.

The third session includes discussion and activities on healthy relationship communication, assertiveness, and appropriate conflict management. Since the program is designed specifically for pregnant female teens, session four concludes with stress, coping, and time management skills tailored for use as participants become mothers.

Adolescents exposed to IPV are also at heightened risk for ADV involvement. *Moms & Teens for Safe Dates* (MTSD; Foshee, Benefield, et al., 2015) is a program specifically designed for nonoffending parent survivors of IPV and their adolescents (Table 5). The program includes six mailed booklets of ADV prevention information and interactive activities. The overall goals of MTSD are to facilitate caregiver–adolescent engagement to increase parental monitoring and family cohesion, decrease caregiver–adolescent conflict, and reduce adolescent acceptance of ADV.

Table 5
Overview of Moms and Teens for Safe Dates Program

Booklet	Goals	Sample activities	Targets
Getting started[a]: Introducing Moms to the *Moms and Teens for Safe Dates* Program	To explain to mothers of teens how to do the program; address specific challenges that they may face in doing the program, based on having been a victim themselves of domestic violence; congratulate the mother on leaving an abusive partner; provide her with tips for healing and staying safe; describe ways of interacting with her adolescent that facilitate and block communication; offer suggestions for how she can encourage adolescent program participation, and address constructs related to motivating and facilitating her engagement in the program.	Mothers complete a true/false assessment that taps into ADV myths and realities.	Mother's perceived severity of ADV Mother's perceived susceptibility of her adolescent to ADV Mother's response efficacy for preventing ADV Mother's self-efficacy for talking to her adolescent about ADV Mother's knowledge of ADV Mother's acceptance of ADV
Booklet 1: Talking About Dating	To improve communication between the mother and adolescent so that they can more comfortably talk about ADV and date rape, in later booklets.	A card game that helps mothers understand current adolescent dating practices and helps adolescents realize what dating was like for their mother. A communication checklist is completed after each activity to indicate which tips for successful communication and communication blockers, mothers and adolescents used in activity discussions.	Mother's skills for communicating with her adolescent Adolescent's conflict resolution skill

Table 5 Continued

Booklet	Goals	Sample activities	Targets
Booklet 2: How You Feel & How You Deal: Skills for Handling Conflict	To increase mother and adolescent skills for diffusing and dealing with anger and settling disagreements.	Families are taught skills for settling disagreements through the acronym SAFE (stay calm, ask questions, find out feelings, and exchange ideas for possible solutions). Families identify the SAFE skills used in a scripted role-play of an adolescent dating couple settling a disagreement.	Mother's skills for communicating with her adolescent. Mother's communication skills with adolescent Adolescent's conflict resolution skills
Booklet 3: Now I See: Recognizing Dating Abuse	To increase mother and adolescent awareness of the various types of ADV; harmful consequences of ADV; and manipulation tactics used by abusers, to "inoculate" the adolescent from those controlling tactics; and to introduce the adolescent to healthy dating characteristics.	Mothers and adolescents discuss how holding traditional stereotypes of men and women led to dating abuse depicted in various scenarios. Adolescents complete a comic strip replacing an abusive reaction to conflict with a date from earlier scenarios with nonabusive and respectful ways of responding to the conflict.	Mother's knowledge of ADV Adolescent's acceptance of ADV Adolescent's perception of negative consequences of ADV Adolescent's conflict resolution skills Adolescent's gender stereotyping
Booklet 4: Preventing Dating Sexual Abuse and Rape	To challenge certain date rape myths and beliefs; increase mother's and adolescent's awareness of sexual dating abuse and its harmful consequences; learn strategies to prevent being a perpetrator or victim of sexual ADV; and learn about date rape drugs (including alcohol).	Mothers and adolescents read scenarios of sexual dating abuse situations and discuss questions about the manipulation tactics used by the perpetrators, signs that the victims did not want to have sex, and potential negative consequences of the rape for the perpetrators and victims.	Mother's knowledge of sexual ADV Adolescent's acceptance of sexual ADV Adolescent's perception of negative consequences of sexual ADV
Booklet 5: Ready, Set, Date! Planning for the Future	To help adolescents think about their goals for treating and being treated by date partners; identify warning signs of ADV; develop a plan with the mother for what to do if they are being treated disrespectfully by a date partner or if they are treating a date disrespectfully; and help families develop guidelines and rules about dating.	Adolescents and mothers work together to develop a plan for what to do if the adolescent is being abused or is abusing dates. Families work together to develop guidelines for dating which are posted on the refrigerator.	Mother's date rule setting and monitoring Mother's belief in the importance of being involved in her adolescent's dating Adolescent's conflict resolution skills

Note. Adapted from Foshee, Dixon, et al., 2015. ADV = adolescent dating violence. [a]This getting-starting booklet is for mothers only.

Expect Respect Support Groups (Ball et al., 2012) is a unique component of a broader school-based cross-cutting violence prevention model for youths exposed to community violence. This curriculum includes five multisession units. Each group session follows a structure of check-in (approximately 5 minutes), didactic presentation (approximately 15 minutes), group activity and discussion (approximately 30 minutes), and wrap-up (approximately 5 minutes). Activities are presented in a variety of media, such as videos, games, role-plays, theater exercises, and art expression. Groups are single-sex (males and females) and facilitated by same-sex leaders to enhance felt safety, openness, and trust in the group.

Information on training, implementation, and costs associated with the comprehensive Expect Respect program is available at https://www.safeaustin.org/our-services/prevention-and-education/expect-respect/. Briefly, ERSGs include the following five units: (1) developing group skills; (2) choosing equality and respect (e.g., characteristics of healthy and unhealthy relationships, use of power, gender stereotypes); (3) recognizing abusive relationships (e.g., naming violence, identify warning signs of violence, recognizing consequences of violence); (4) learning skills for healthy relationships (e.g., managing jealousy and conflict, consent, setting boundaries, resolving); and (5) getting the message out (e.g., standing up against violence).

DePrince and colleagues tested the efficacy of two different theory-driven programs: *Risk Detection/Executive Function* and *Social Learning/Feminist intervention* (DePrince et al., 2015) designed to reduce revictimization for female youths with a history of maltreatment and foster care placement (Table 6). Neither condition emerged as superior to the other, suggesting that both provide effective, viable prevention options to high-risk female youths.

Individual health behaviors can also increase risk for ADV. Designed to address risk for sexual assault perpetration among high-risk heavy-drinking college men, *Sexual Assault and Alcohol Feedback and Education* (SAFE) was developed by Orchowski and colleagues (2018). This program consists of three sessions varying in length from 90 minutes to 2.5 hrs. Intervention targets include addressing the pharmacological effects of alcohol by enhancing substance use harm reduction strategies, targeting maladaptive alcohol expectancies, and providing psychoeducation on overlapping underpinnings of alcohol use and ADV. Sessions are delivered in a motivational interviewing style and cover topics such as alcohol use and sexual activity, peer norms, empathy, masculinity, consent, and prosocial bystander behaviors. Session one is delivered individually, session two is a group-based workshop, and session three serves as a review and skills practice administered by two male facilitators (Table 7 and Table 8).

Table 6
Theoretical Approaches to Revictimization and Associated Intervention Targets

Approach	Process	Intervention target
Social learning or feminist theories	Violent tactics are acceptable and even effective routes to resolving conflict.	Understanding power and its role in relationship violence.
	Problems in assertiveness and communication skills.	Develop skills to build healthy relationships and to recognize and respond to abuse in their own relationships.
	Develop expectations that relationships will include harm.	
	Socialization of gender roles and sexism that support power discrepancies and violence.	Understand the societal influences and pressures that can lead to violence; develop skills to respond.
Risk detection and executive function	Fail to notice external danger cues (e.g., something in the environment, such as the expression on another person's face).	Increase executive functioning in the environment (directing attention).
	Fail to notice internal danger cues (e.g., one's own feelings of fear).	Increase executive functioning for emotions; improve emotion labeling and awareness.
	Notice cue(s) but fail to maintain and use this information, or become distracted; thus, multiple danger cues seem disconnected and unrelated.	Increase working memory, interference control.
	Notice danger and know what to do, but fail to change or inhibit current behaviors.	Increase set shifting; inhibition.
	Notice danger but have difficulty generating possible behavioral responses.	Increase cognitive flexibility, knowledge of possible responses.
	Have difficulty planning or initiating a response.	Increase planning, practice generating ways to respond.
Nonspecific processes (common to both approaches)	Violence in intimate relationships viewed as acceptable.	Decrease acceptability of dating violence.
	Deficits in assertiveness skills increase conflict and aggression in intimate relationships.	Increase assertiveness skills.

Note. Reprinted with permission from DePrince et al., 2015, p. 534.

Table 7
Sexual Assault and Alcohol Feedback and Education (SAFE) Intervention Targets

Intervention target	Objective
Pharmacological effects	Enhance utilization of strategies to limit drinking; enhance protective behavioral strategies to reduce alcohol-related consequences; increase awareness of alcohol myopia as an influence on sexual behavior and bystander intervention; increase awareness of the likelihood of misperceiving sexual intent, especially if the dating partner has been drinking
Alcohol expectancies	Increase awareness of personal alcohol expectancies related to power, satisfaction; increase awareness of how expectancies influence sexual behavior and bystander intervention; debunk use of alcohol as a justification for sexual violence
Shared influences on alcohol use and aggression	Increase awareness of how alcohol use is associated with perceptions of traditional masculine norms; debunk misperceptions of the extent to which other men engage in sexual activity when intoxicated; reduce adherence to rape myths; increase empathy toward victims of sexual violence

Note. Adapted from Orchowski et al., 2018, p. 1376.

Table 8
Sexual Assault and Alcohol Feedback and Education (SAFE) Session Components and Aims

Component	Aim
Session 1	
Rapport building	Establish rapport through empathic, concerned, nonauthoritarian, and nonjudgmental conversation.
Exploration of participant behaviors	Gather information about participant's alcohol use and sexual behavior; outline how alcohol use is involved in the participant's recent sexual activity.
Identify pros/cons	Help the participant to identify both positive and negative aspects to alcohol use, sexual behaviors, and sexual activity involving alcohol; highlight discrepancies between these behaviors and their goals and values.

Provide personalized feedback	Personalized information on:
	• Personal alcohol use in relation to that of their peers
	• Co-occurrence of alcohol use and sexual activity
	• Blood alcohol level (i.e., average, peak, average during sexual activity, peak during sexual activity)
	• General consequences and risks of drinking
	• Alcohol-related sexual consequences
	• Sexual communication and consent
	  – While sober vs. while intoxicated
	  – Discuss potential effects of expectancies and alcohol myopia
	• Utilization of bystander intervention strategies
	  – While sober vs. while intoxicated
	  – Discuss potential effects of expectancies and alcohol myopia.

Discuss motivation to change	Attempt to elicit change talk for drinking and sexual behaviors, and enhance participant commitment to change.

Table 8   Continued

Component	Aim
Discuss barriers to change	Increase self-efficacy for change by discussing potential barriers that might serve as roadblocks during the change process.
Discuss strategies for change	Provide guidance to participant in setting goals for reducing problems related to drinking and its role in sexual activity, consent, and/or bystander intervention.
Session 2	
Definitions and facts	Increase men's knowledge on the prevalence of sexual assault on college campuses.
Social norms	Correct men's misperceptions regarding sexual behavior and alcohol use through the provision of social norms.
False accusations of sexual assault	Correct men's misperceptions regarding the frequency of false accusations of sexual assault, and to increase men's empathy regarding the effects of sexual assault.
Sexual communication and consent	Provide information and create discussion to help men in understanding the conditions of sexual consent.
Bystander intervention	Highlight ways men can increase their awareness of risk of sexually aggressive behavior among peers, discuss personal use of bystander intervention strategies, and practice strategies to intervene when witnessing dating and/or sexual violence.
Session 3	
Utilization of program content	Discuss understanding of sexual assault on campus since participating in the program and create a discussion for how men have noticed applying program content in their lives since participating.
Sexual communication and consent	Create a discussion on men's perception of the consent model and alcohol's influence in sexual situations.
Correct misperceived social norms	Create discussion on norms supportive of sexual violence, including perceptions of traditionally masculine behaviors.
Bystander intervention	Discuss personal engagement in bystander intervention over the interim. Role-play a bystander intervention scenario and garner feedback on this approach from men.
Small group practice	Present scenarios to men and have them identify verbal and nonverbal strategies to intervene.

Note. Adapted from Orchowski et al., 2018, p. 1377–1378.

Tertiary

Tertiary prevention seeks to reduce the severity or duration of ADV perpetration or victimization among teens already involved with ADV.

ADV Interventions Designed for Perpetrators

Men Stopping Violence (Salazar & Cook, 2006) is a gender-specific and culturally tailored program to meet the needs of adjudicated (i.e., incarcerated juveniles) African American/Black male adolescents (Table 9). The program is five sessions in duration and guided by feminist theory.

Table 9
Overview of *Men Stopping Violence* Intervention

Session	Objectives	Activities
1: Stage setting (2 hrs)	Gain awareness of the beliefs on which men base their choices to assault women (e.g., "women provoke male violence," "women exaggerate, lie and make false accusations about men," and "women, given the chance will be sexually unfaithful").	Present excerpt from the 1995 movie *Dead Presidents*, in which an African American war veteran blames his partner for provoking him, lying, and for being unfaithful. He in turn physically assaults her. Participants are asked to explain the character's reasoning, whether he was justified, and how they would respond if the woman were their mother or sister.
	Learn that men and boys can respectfully disagree with one another for the purpose of deepening their level of learning.	During discussion, facilitators model respectful and appropriate behavior. Specifically, they show how adult men confront other men and boys in a respectful manner, and how men routinely blame and hold women and girls responsible for the ways men think, feel, and act.
	Prepare to attend the next four sessions of the program.	Describe the classroom format and explain that batterers are attending classes to take responsibility for their violence.
2: The Court Class (2 hrs)	Learn that men are responsible for battering women and that men are responsible for stopping these assaults.	Facilitators provide a didactic presentation on the profile of men who assault women and why men choose to assault women. Facilitators provide exercises in which participants name the tactics men employ to control women. Emphasis is placed on those tactics that illustrate a pattern of intentionally controlling behavior rather than random acts of abuse. Courthouse setting underscores how adult men are being held accountable for their criminal behavior.
	Learn how violence committed against women by men is analogous to White acts of violence against people of color and to heterosexual acts of violence against LGBTQ people.	Facilitators provide information regarding the connection between racism and sexism. Facilitators define oppression and engage participants in discussion of the commonalties among the mistreatment of people of color by Whites, the mistreatment of women by men, and the mistreatment of LGBTQ by heterosexuals.

Table 9 Continued

Session	Objectives	Activities
3 and 4: The Batterers Intervention Classes (2 hrs each + 30-minute introduction)	Learn that men can take responsibility for their abuse of women and that men can stop the abuse if they choose to.	Facilitators provide opportunity to observe men working to change their abusive behaviors by respectfully challenging each other to listen without interrupting and to take seriously the other person's point of view. Facilitators provided situations where the participants experienced the men holding each other accountable for their abuse by imposing meaningful consequences. For example, if a man committed an abusive act while in the program, one consequence would be to provide the facilitators, his classmates, and his partner with a written description of the most recent and the worst incident of abuse against that partner. Participants experienced men examining belief systems regarding prescribed gender roles that motivated them to assault their partners (e.g., "Women don't go out at night without their husbands, so men have the right to block them physically from leaving to pursue friendships or work outside the home").
5: Review	Participants learn that all men, youths, and adults are responsible for stopping assaults against women and girls.	Facilitators provide participants opportunities to describe and discuss what they learned about batterers and about themselves from the men in the classes. Facilitators provide participants with a scenario in which a young man and his date encounter another couple where the boy is assaulting the girl. The participants were asked, "What would you think? What would you feel? What would you do?"
	Participants learn that boys' choices to degrade girls are rooted in attitudes of contempt and in traditional gender roles and are related to other forms of oppression.	Facilitators and participants list terms for boys and for girls that illustrate double standards (e.g., boys alleged to "sleep around" are called studs, whereas girls who allegedly sleep around are called sluts). The typical or characteristic disparaging terms for girls such as "stupid," "lazy," and "liars" are compared with the disparaging terms for people of color. Facilitators conclude with a quote: "Just as ending racism is painful life-long work, so is ending the sexism that drives assaults on women and girls by men and boys."

Note. Based on Salazar & Cook, 2006.

Real Talk (Rothman et al., 2020) is designed as a motivational interview-style intervention delivered in health care settings. It is a single-session 30- to 45-minute intervention delivered by trained community members (nonclinicians). Real Talk proceeds through 10 steps, consistent with a screening, brief intervention, and referral to treatment (SBIRT) model: (1) establishing rapport, (2) eliciting information about dating abuse perpetration, (3) providing tailored feedback, (4) assessing readiness to change, (5) reviewing healthy relationships choices, (6) contemplating the pros and cons of behavior change, (7) identifying barrier to change, (8) reassessing readiness to change, (9) making referrals to desired resources, and (10) supportive booster calls during the 6 weeks after intervention delivery.

ADV Interventions Designed for Victims

Many community agencies offer evidence-based treatment for adolescent victims of sexual or interpersonal violence. Although there is robust research evidence for the use of trauma treatments to address adolescent and young adult PTSD (e.g., trauma-focused cognitive behavioral therapy, Cohen et al., 2012; and cognitive processing therapy, Resick et al., 2016), fewer interventions have been developed and empirically tested to specifically prevent ADV or sexual assault revictimization. We highly recommend practitioners review gold standard evidence-based PTSD, MDD, or GAD (and other) treatments for victims of ADV presenting with clear diagnostic indications.

In some areas of the United States, adolescents can also request protection orders, issued when an individual provides reasonable proof of stalking, physical ADV victimization, sexual ADV victimization, and in limited cases, psychological ADV. Such "stay-away" orders can require that the perpetrator be prohibited from contact (via phone, online, or in-person), required to always maintain a certain distance from victim, be restricted from participating in school events when the victim is present, and be prohibited from visiting the victim at home or in their place of employment. States with strong civil protection policies see lower rates of ADV (Hoefer et al., 2015). However, actual access to protection orders for dating youth is variable and difficult to ascertain, as most states fail to provide clear circumstances under which teens are granted these abilities (e.g., operationalizing what defines a relationship, if a minor can seek such an order, if the order can be sought against another minor, when a minor can represent themselves in court, if parental notification is required, and considerations for same-sex couples).

In addition to the previously reviewed efforts by DePrince and colleagues (2015), the *Date Skills to Manage Aggression in Relationships for Teens* (Date SMART) program targets ADV and sexual risk behavior among adolescent girls with a prior history of physical ADV exposure. Developers of the intervention describe it as trauma-informed and based on the principles of cognitive behavior therapy (CBT). Date SMART consists of six weekly 2-hr group sessions, followed by a single booster session 6 weeks later. The intervention is skills-based and aims to equip youth with tools to navigate risky situations around relationship aggression and unprotected sex. Date SMART is based on assumed skills deficits that increase risk for ADV and risky sexual behaviors among adolescent females, specifically targeting difficulties with depressive symptoms, self-regulation, and interpersonal effectiveness.

The Date SMART program provides psychoeducation and includes self-assessment, cognitive restructuring, problem solving, assertive communication, self-soothing, and emotion regulation strategies for negative affect. Importantly, the program offers skills training for adaptive regulation of thoughts and emotions early in the curriculum, so that participants are equipped with these strategies when navigating potentially triggering material during the program itself. Specifically, the seven Date SMART intervention sessions include aspects of the following: (1) healthy and unhealthy relationships and behaviors, SMART problems solving, and CBT model of emotions; (2) safety planning and cognitive restructuring; (3) managing anger and jealousy, emotional thermometer, and mindfulness; (4) managing depression, changing unhealthy thoughts, communication skills; (5) continued communication skills, sexual communication; (6) social support and relationship values; (7) skills review, empowerment (Rizzo et al., 2018).

4.2.3   ADV Prevention Implementation: Where

Beyond school settings, ADV interventions may be implemented in hospitals, community clinics, and correctional facilities. Delivering interventions in schools is attractive for several reasons, including easy access to large groups of adolescents, as well as campus- and district-level infrastructure for program delivery. However, school-based programs potentially miss important clusters of adolescents. Chronic absenteeism (due to truancy, homelessness, incarceration, unreliable transportation, etc.) affects 14% to 20% of US adolescents, with higher rates among racial and ethnic minority and low-income populations (US Department of Education, 2019). Consequently, community, correctional, or health care–based activities may capture different subsets of adolescents experiencing, or at risk for, ADV.

School-Based ADV programs

Notably, the vast majority of empirically tested ADV programs are school-based and universal. Below, we review a nonexhaustive list of the many options designed for classroom-based delivery.

Among the best-known school-based interventions is *Safe Dates* (Foshee et al., 1996; 1998). Supported by evidence from among the first randomized controlled trials (RCTs) of ADV prevention among adolescents, Safe Dates' curriculum of ten 45-minute sessions is taught by health and physical education teachers (Table 10). In addition to these lessons, Safe Dates involves a theater production performed by adolescent peers and culminates in a participant poster contest wherein adolescents are encouraged to create original ADV prevention posters and vote on the best posters on their campus. Community engagement is included by providing workshops to community service providers across disciplines (e.g., social workers, physicians and medical staff, mental health professionals, school counselors, and police departments).

Table 10

Teaching Objectives of the Safe Dates Prevention Curriculum

Lesson	Objective
Day 1: Defining caring relationships	• Promote students' consideration of the qualities that are most important to them in dating relationships. • Discuss ways that people act to show they care. • Draw out characteristics that are similar in all caring relationships, romantic and platonic. • Promote the students' consideration of how they want to be treated by a dating partner and how they want to treat a dating partner. • Emphasize that students have a choice in how they are treated in a dating relationship and how they treat their partners.
Day 2: Defining dating abuse	• Describe dating behaviors that can be harmful. • Differentiate between harmful and abusive behaviors. • Differentiate and define physically and emotionally abusive behaviors. • Discuss facts about dating abuse.
Day 3: Why do people abuse?	• Discuss the roles of manipulation, power, and control in dating abuse. • Challenge the attribution that violence from jealousy indicates love. • Demonstrate that a person's feelings, actions, and thinking can be a target for abusive control. • Foster an awareness of consequences of both physical and emotional abuse. • Outline warning signs for abuse.
Day 4: How to help friends	• Demonstrate the reasons that people do not or cannot "just leave" an abusive relationship. • Acknowledge the difficulties in seeking help as a victim of ADV. • Describe different methods of giving help to friends who are in abusive relationships. • Describe community resources. • Encourage people who are victims of abuse and perpetrators of abuse to seek help.
Day 5: Helping friends	• Discuss the red flags for being a perpetrator and a victim of dating abuse. • Have students practice talking to a friend who is violent toward their dating partner. • Have students practice talking to a friend who is being abused by their dating partner. • Equip students with the skills to confront dating abuse with their peers.
Day 6: Images of relationships	• Increase awareness that our images of dating relationships influence how we treat, and are treated by, our dating partners. • Increase students' understanding of how their images of relationships are created. • Define gender stereotyping. • Explain how gender stereotyping can influence images and dating interactions. • Illustrate the link between gender stereotyping and dating abuse.
Day 7: Equal power through communication	• Describe eight communication skills that can be helpful in resolving conflict. • Give students an opportunity to practice their communication skills. • Give students an opportunity to think about nonviolent strategies to use when their girlfriend or boyfriend does not use communication skills.

Table 10 Continued

Lesson	Objective
Day 8: How we feel; How we deal	• Discuss the importance of acknowledging feelings. • Provide the students with an extended list of words that describe feelings. • Acknowledge anger as a powerful and valid emotion. • Facilitate a discussion of hot buttons, cues to anger, and nonabusive response to anger. • Emphasize that the way one responds to anger is a choice.
Day 9: Sexual assault	• Define sexual assault. • Discourage victim blaming for rape. • Promote proscribed rape norms rather than prescribed rape norms. • Illustrate verbal and nonverbal cues that indicate someone is unsure or not ready to have sex. • Promote the use of self-defense techniques in potential rape situations. • Encourage students to be clear with their dating partners about their sexual boundaries. • Discuss ways to reduce the risk of rape in a dating situation.
Day 10: Summary and poster contest	• Obtain student feedback on the curriculum. • Describe the poster contest.

Note. Reprinted with permission from Foshee et al., 1996, p. 46. ADV = adolescent dating violence.

Another school-based program, *Ending Violence* (Jaycox et al., 2006), comprises three classroom lessons focused on legal issues surrounding ADV. The program is based on social learning theory and teaches youths about ADV, healthy relationships, and legal rights (emphasizing that legal protections both support victims and punish perpetrators of ADV). Ending Violence is taught by attorneys, with the goal of increasing students' comfort level in reaching out and speaking with attorneys, as well as helping them better understand their legal rights and how to exercise them. The Ending Violence curriculum (Jaycox et al., 2006) can be divided into three parts. The first hour includes information on the types of, warning signs for, and prevalence of ADV, as well as why it is difficult for victims to leave a violent relationship. The second hour includes information on the legal aspects of ADV, including criminal versus legal justice systems and restraining orders. Finally, the third hour involves the restraining order process (including role-playing the court process) and discusses safety planning.

The *Katie Brown Educational Program* (KBEP; Joppa et al., 2016) is a brief, manualized school-based ADV intervention for high school health classes of up to 35 students. The program consists of five sessions (50–60 minutes each) designed to be administered in a single school week. This program is based in social learning theory, utilizing observational learning, discussion, role-plays, and modeling of healthy relationship skills to communicate content. Each lesson includes a didactic lecture, group discussion, individual activities, and worksheets. Content covered in KBEP includes identifying ADV, relationship rights, self-esteem, conflict resolution, communication skills, healthy relationships, personal responsibility, stereotypes and media portrayals of gender roles, the cycle of violence, and ADV warning signs. KBEP can be integrated into existing high school health curricula. Program strengths include its brevity, discussion of coeducational issues related to gender stereotypes, and portrayal of males and females both as potential perpetrators and victims of ADV.

Community-Based Interventions

SafERteens (Cunningham et al., 2009) is a hospital-based emergency department intervention for alcohol misuse and peer violence, including ADV, among adolescents (Table 11). Rooted in motivational interviewing, this program has been tested using two delivery formats: computer-only and therapist plus computer combination administration. Elements across both delivery formats were designed to enhance motivation and self-efficacy for behavior change, emphasize personal choice and responsibility, highlight the difference between maladaptive current behaviors and their desired goals and values (i.e., develop discrepancy), and increase adolescents' problem recognition. SafERteens also involves skills training for effective alcohol refusal, healthy conflict resolution, and anger management via role-plays. The intervention is brief, made up of a single session of up to 35 minutes long.

For youths who report ADV involvement, intervention content in SafERteens is tailored to directly address ADV prevention strategies during role-plays. Specifically, in the combined administration, the computer program prompts therapists to discuss how the adolescents would handle an argument with a dating partner, and therapists walk through the pros and cons of speaking with that partner when one or both partners are drunk or angry. Safety plans are discussed if adolescents report fear of their dating partner. In the computer-only format, the role-play places the participant in a similar situation, in which they are pressured to drink alcohol and confront their angry, intoxicated dating partner during a conflict. The computer delivery is narrated by a cartoon-style "buddy" for the participant to "hang out" with during the session. Notably, the participant chooses a buddy that is gender-, race-, and age-appropriate. The program offers information on increased risk of violence when drinking, encourages options such as waiting to manage conflicts when both dating partners are calm and sober, and reminds adolescents about adaptive emotion regulation strategies. The computer-only delivery also states, "If your partner has hit you before, or you are afraid of him or her, do not talk to the partner alone. Ask someone for help." For all delivery modes, a brochure with numbers for ADV hotlines is given to adolescents at the end of the intervention.

Table 11

Key Elements of *SafERteens* Interventions

Key elements	Goal of element	Content for computer (C), therapist (T), or both (B)
Introduction: agenda setting (~2 minutes)	• Thank individual for participation. • Establish rapport. • Explain purpose of intervention to talk about alcohol and violence.	C: Participant selects Buddy; T: Therapist introduction
Personal goals (~3–5 minutes)	• Review and elaborate on goals and values. • Begin to develop discrepancy between goals and values vs. current behavior, by exploring how drinking and fighting fit in with goals and values.	B: Brief intervention goals listed C: Buddy reiterates goals T: Brief discussion of goals
Personalized feedback: alcohol and violence (~3–5 minutes)	• Review survey responses regarding alcohol, fighting, and weapon carriage. • Compare behaviors with norms for age and sex. • Raise concern by providing feedback on consequences of drinking and fighting. • Continue to develop discrepancy by exploring impact of behavior on goals and values currently and in future. • From a prevention perspective, if behavior is lower level, provide opportunity to think about future behaviors and begin to strengthen commitment to avoid involvement	B: Sex and age-appropriate graphs shown on screen. B: Reviewed (by T or C-Buddy) in a matter-of-fact, nonjudgmental manner. T: Discuss how this currently or in the future could impact goals. C: Ask if thinking affects goals, check response on screen; reflective summary statements provided by Buddy.
Reasons to stay away from drinking and fighting (~3–5 minutes)	• Elicit reasons to change (or maintain for prevention focus) by exploring reasons to stay away from drinking and fighting. • Tip the decisional balance in favor of change. • Elicit and affirm change talk. • Support self-efficacy for making changes. • Continue to develop discrepancy by exploring impact of current behavior on current and future goals and values. • Roll with resistance. • Emphasize participant responsibility for making choices.	B: Reasons for staying away from drinking and fighting presented on screen for participant to check. T: Use motivational interviewing strategies to make a connection between reasons to avoid these behaviors, vs. goals. C: Buddy summarizes the reasons checked on the screen to help make a connection between behaviors and goals.
Safer choices; five role-plays practicing risk reduction (~10–12 minutes)	• Practice five scenarios that were selected by the computer, based on gender and risk profile (e.g., high or low risk for alcohol or violence) obtained from assessment. Role-plays focus on anger management, conflict resolution, avoiding drinking and violent situations, refusal skills for weapon carriage, drinking, binge drinking, and driving or riding under the influence. Each teen interacts with scenarios from these three categories: (1) violence, (2) violence while intoxicated, and (3) alcohol.	T: Role-plays and options are discussed. C: Animated video game style. Character situations viewed. Decision points where participant is given opportunity to choose the next action. Participants may "choose" a negative choice (drinking, fighting); these choices are not viewed. Instead, Buddy gives feedback on consequences and how they might affect goals. Participant chooses a better option, which is then animated.

Table 11 Continued

Key elements	Goal of element	Content for computer (C), therapist (T), or both (B)
Summarized session and closing (~3–5 minutes)	• Provide participant with summary of goals, behaviors, reasons to stay away from drinking and fighting. • Affirm change talk. Strengthen commitment to change. Support self-efficacy. • Review appropriate resources (e.g., mentor, psychological and family services, leisure activities). • Begin to think about change plan by identifying one next step in avoiding drinking, fighting, or weapon carriage.	T: Summary to reinforce change talk; support and advice to develop their plan. Review community resources with an emphasis on linkage addressing specific risk profile. C: Buddy summary of individual goals and reasons checked to stay away from drinking and fighting; encouraging follow-through with community resources handout.

Note. Reprinted with permission from *Academic Emergency Medicine, 16*, R. M. Cunningham et al., Three-month follow-up of brief computerized and therapist interventions for alcohol and violence among teens, p. 1197. © 2009, with permission from John Wiley and Sons.

ADV Programs in Justice-Based and Correctional Settings

Efforts to develop and test ADV interventions with justice-involved adolescents and emerging adults have been exceedingly rare. Potential benefits of intervention with this group extend beyond preventing or mitigating ADV; strong ADV programming for justice-involved youth may contribute to reducing recidivism and lowering the societal and monetary costs of enduring health consequences and continued justice involvement. Leveraging the infrastructure of juvenile justice via probation and related community mental health rehabilitation services is one cost-effective approach to reaching this group. There is an urgent need for accessible and effective ADV intervention programs that meet the unique needs of high-risk, justice-involved youth.

In addition to work by Salazar and Cook (2006) to engage justice-involved males (reviewed earlier in this chapter in the section ADV Interventions Designed for Perpetrators), Kelly and colleagues (2007) created an intervention to address the sexual health and ADV needs of high-risk female adolescents in juvenile justice. The *Girl Talk-2* intervention is a 6-hr program delivered in 3-hr blocks across 2 days. A unique component of Girl Talk-2 is its use of peer educators – women of similar ethnic, racial, and economic backgrounds to those of the adolescent program participants. Peer educators themselves engage in a 3-hr training. The program is based on social cognitive theory and covers topics of sexually transmitted infections and HIV, the need for routine gynecological care (i.e., pap smears, pelvic examinations, screenings), condom use, local resources, and communication skills related to ADV risk reduction and conflict management (e.g., brainstorming solutions, validating partner, asking questions). Program activities include journaling, role-plays, condom demonstrations, group discussions, and one-to-one conversations between participants and peer educators.

While rare, ADV interventions for justice-involved youth have potential to reduce recidivism and long-term harm

4.2.4   ADV Prevention Implementation: When

Developmentally, programs delivered earlier in adolescence are likely to differ in content and scope from those offered in late adolescence and emerging adulthood. Thus, we offer example programs across the developmental period of adolescence (i.e., *When*) to illustrate similarities and differences in curricula as youths grow older.

Early Adolescence

Targeting early adolescents, *Me & You* (Peskin et al., 2019) is a healthy relationships curriculum comprising 13 classroom and computer-based lessons with parent–child take-home activities and teacher training that focuses on promoting healthy relationships and explicitly addressing unhealthy dating behavior, including emotional, physical, sexual, and cyber dating abuse. The Me & You curriculum includes the following classroom-, computer-, and classroom/computer hybrid-based lessons (classroom and computer), shown in Box 2.

Box 2 Me & You Lessons
Classroom-based lessons
• Introduction to curriculum, personal strengths, and building healthy relationships • Identifying personal rules, and challenges to those rules • Defining active consent, warning signs of dating violence, gender role stereotypes • Skills for managing emotions and communicating • Curriculum review and additional skills practice
Computer-based lessons
• Characteristics of healthy and unhealthy friendships • Recognize connection between thoughts and feelings, skills for managing emotions • Protecting personal rules in the context of technology-related communication • Types of dating violence • Classroom/computer hybrid–based lessons • Refusal skills (clear "no"s and alternative actions) • Effective communication strategies, skills practice • Getting out of unhealthy relationships, accessing social support and resources

Midadolescence

Most rigorously tested interventions have been designed and implemented with adolescents between the ages of 14 and 18, typically delivered in high school settings. *Connections: Relationships and Marriage* (Gardner et al.,

2004; Gardner & Boellaard, 2007) is one relationship education curriculum developed for high school adolescents that underscores how teenage dating dynamics can set a foundation for healthy marriages long-term. Totaling 15 one-hour school-based lessons, this curriculum covers four units (i.e., personality, relationships, communication, and marriage). While not explicitly religiously affiliated, practitioners should be thoughtful when applying this program to culturally diverse groups, given its heavy emphasis on heterosexual monogamous marriage concepts.

Late Adolescence and Emerging Adulthood

Research evidence around effective ADV intervention for late adolescents and emerging adults is dominated by college student samples and largely designed to be administered in university campus settings. Thus, effective prevention and intervention strategies for community youths outside of higher education is an area in dire need of more research. A recent systematic review and meta-analysis identified over 29 programs designed to address ADV specifically (i.e., not focused solely on partying or sexual assault) among college students (Wong et al., 2023). Results indicated that although programs were effective overall at increasing bystander efficacy and intentions, ADV knowledge, and prosocial attitudes around ADV, those programs were not effective at increasing actual bystander behaviors.

Another prominent evidence-based program is *Green Dot*, a bystander program developed by Dorothy J. Edwards. Please note that we review the theoretical basis of bystander interventions with additional program examples under the Primary Prevention subsection (Section 4.2.2 ADV Prevention Implementation: What). *Green Dot* aims to train and mobilize potential bystanders to effectively intervene with peers involved in ADV. This is done by encouraging and empowering bystanders to engage in effective behaviors after the fact (e.g., helping victims of ADV), as well as taking proactive measures at the time of an ADV incident (e.g., safely interacting with aggressive or at-risk peers to mitigate violence).

Green Dot comprises two primary activities: a 50-minute motivational speech in introductory college courses and orientation sessions, followed by intensive staff-led bystander training. The speech introduces and emphasizes being an active and responsive bystander and aims to empower students with the knowledge that intervening can be simple and effective at preventing ADV. The intensive bystander training involves teaching and practicing specific safe bystander behaviors. Training is administered in groups of 20 to 25 students and ranges from 4 to 6 hrs in duration. This training is advertised on campuses for voluntary campus-wide participation, with concerted recruitment efforts made through nominations by peers, faculty, and staff of students perceived as particularly influential. In this way, leaders of informal campus social networks are targeted, trained, and able to informally disseminate their knowledge to the broader campus community. Identified influential student leaders receive personal training invitations from the university provost. Information on costs, training, and implementation of Green Dot can be accessed at https://alteristic.org/services/green-dot/.

4.2.5 ADV Prevention Implementation: How

Presentation formats (i.e., *How*) also differ; some interventions are delivered in groups, whereas others focus on individual or parent–child sessions. Given the importance of peer influence on adolescent sexuality and dating (Arriaga & Foshee, 2004; Maheux et al., 2020), group-based programs may be especially beneficial for ADV interventions, as adolescents can receive peer feedback and support.

More broadly, group treatments are theorized to cultivate a sense of belonging among members and enhance self-reflection via interacting with others facing similar challenges. However, some evidence suggests that aggregating homogenous groups of antisocial adolescents may exacerbate aggressive and deviant tendencies (Dishion et al., 1999). Thus, group-based formats targeting high-risk, similar adolescents may increase risk for iatrogenic increases in violent behavior. Individual sessions may circumvent some of these concerns and include the potential for more personalization and tailored practice of materials and skills. However, individual therapy among violence-affected adolescents can be less cost-effective than group paradigms. Parent–child sessions are also a compelling format, given findings that parent-level variables (e.g., parental acceptance of aggression, interparental conflict, and parent–child relationship quality) predict ADV (Jouriles et al., 2012; Miller et al., 2009). As such, providing parents and their children resources to discuss and support healthy dating behaviors may be particularly successful.

Classroom-Based Interventions

The Fourth R is a universal, classroom-based program that teaches healthy relationship skills to prevent violence

The *Fourth R* is an intensive classroom-based intervention including group discussion, role-play, and application activities (e.g., guided research projects) developed to promote well-being and healthy peer relationships among adolescents by addressing often co-occurring problems of ADV, mental health, and substance misuse. Fourth R is rooted in the idea that relationships are integral to adaptive development and that high-risk adolescent behaviors tend to co-occur within peer relationships. Leveraging social cognitive theory, the developers also conceptualize healthy relationship skills as something that can be taught, learned, rehearsed, and enhanced. Thus, beyond **R**eading, w**R**iting, and a**R**ithmetic, students need education and skills training on healthy **R**elationships. Importantly, Fourth R is universal in nature – so that all students in a particular class, grade, or school receive the intervention. This approach has the benefit of not stigmatizing and grouping together "high risk" children, while also promoting healthy relationship behaviors in all students regardless of risk for violence.

Originally designed and tested with Canadian ninth-grade students (Wolfe et al., 2009), Fourth R has since been adapted and tested with middle school American youths (Temple et al., 2021). Multiple adaptations include developmentally appropriate changes to content and cultural references (see https://youthrelationships.org/ for additional information). Fourth R is delivered by classroom teachers, comprising three units, each with seven to eight classroom sessions of approximately 75 minutes each (Table 12).

Table 12

Fourth R Units, Lessons, and Example Content From the Middle School Version[a]

Lesson	Example content
Unit 1: Personal safety and injury prevention	
1. Healthy relationships	Qualities of a good friend
2. Impact of bullying and harassment	Understanding the bully, being bullied, and the bystander
3. Benefits and dangers of technology	Safe and responsible use of technology
4. Stress and emotional regulation	Identifying stressors and coping activities
5. Decision making	IDEAL decision-making model (**I**dentify the problem, **D**escribe how you might solve the problem, **E**valuate all possible solutions, **A**ct on one solution, **L**earn from your choices)
6. Skills into practice	Identifying passive, aggressive, and assertive communication
7. Practicing Skills and culminating activity	Delay, refusal, negotiation skills, and assertive communication practice
Unit 2: Substance use, addictions, and related behaviors	
8. Problematic substance use	Internal and external factors of substance use
9. Linking substance use with mental health	Discussion about connection between mental health and substance use
10. Connection between body image and substance use	Short-term and long-term effects of common substance use
11. Help-seeking practice	Help seeking and listening and supporting skills
12. Researching the implications of substance use and addictions	Impact on family and friends, legal, health, and safety
13. Implications of substance use and addictions presentations	Understanding impact of substance use and addictions
14. Practicing skills related to substance use and other addictions	Delay, refusal, and negotiation skills
15. Practicing skills and culminating activity	Role-play exercises
Unit 3: Human development and sexual health	
16. Knowing yourself	Values, goals, and other factors that influence decisions
17. STI/STDs research	Symptoms and prevention
18. Preventing STI/STDs	Student presentations on STI/STDs
19. Factors related to sexual health decisions	Scenarios and discussion

Table 12 Continued

Lesson	Example content
20. Consent	What is consent and when consent is and is not being communicated
21. Communication	Communication with your partner, delay, refusal, and negotiation skills
22. Culminating activity	Written assessment

Note. Based on Temple et al., 2021, p. 4. [a]There is an optional unit on healthy eating.

Individual ADV Programs

Miller and colleagues (2015) tested an individual ADV program administered in school health centers titled the *School Health Center Healthy Adolescent Relationships Program* (SHARP). The curriculum consists of clinical guidelines, 21 training slides for clinicians, and a brochure on healthy relationships, help seeking, and ADV resources. The program involves a 3-hr training on the intervention, including how to introduce the brochure to students, conduct an ADV assessment, and provide effective referrals to victim services when necessary.

Importantly, the SHARP program functions by having providers discuss the brochure on every encounter, regardless of the reason for the health clinic visit. For students who do not disclose ADV, brochures are still offered to send to peers. Reviewing the brochure takes less than 1 minute, with longer discussions as needed following disclosures of ADV. Beyond the brochure, each health clinic campus utilizes youth advisory boards that organize and host school-wide events to facilitate ADV outreach and encourage students to visit the student health center.

Parent–Child Interventions

ADV interventions designed for caregivers and youths are limited. We reviewed Moms and Teens for Safe Dates (Foshee, Benefield, et al., 2015) as well as JOVEN (Gonzalez-Guarda et al., 2015) earlier in this chapter (see 4.2.2 ADV Prevention Implementation: What), both of which include caregiver components. Additionally, Families for Safe Dates (Foshee et al., 2012) is the program from which Moms and Teens for Safe Dates was adapted; thus, they share heavy overlap in program content.

Indirect and Online Programs

Teen Choices (Levesque et al., 2016), an online program delivered across three 25- to 30-minute sessions, is individually tailored based on an assessment of an adolescent's dating history, including ADV involvement and stage of readiness for using healthy relationship skills. The program is fully computerized, thus offering guaranteed treatment fidelity. Based on the transtheoretical model (i.e., stages of change), Teen Choices facilitates learning and motivation for using five core healthy relationship skills:

1. Trying to understand and respect the other person's feelings and needs
2. Using calm, nonviolent ways to deal with disagreements
3. Respecting the other person's boundaries
4. Communicating feelings and needs clearly and respectfully
5. Making decisions that you know are good for you in relationships

Youths already in relationships are encouraged to apply these skills with dating partners. Youths who have yet to date are encouraged to practice these skills with platonic peers as a foundation for healthy relationships with future romantic partners. For youths reporting ADV victimization and active fear of partner, Teen Choices pivots away from focusing on healthy relationship skills and instead seeks to support youths in staying safe in their relationship.

To avoid unintended increases in self-blame, *staying safe* is operationally defined within Teen Choices as (1) getting help, (2) making a safety plan, and (3) deciding whether the relationship is right for you. A notable strength of Teen Choices is its individual tailoring based on adolescent risk level; five content tracks cover the needs of high-risk victims, high-risk daters, low-risk daters, high-risk nondating teens, and low-risk nondating teens, based on student responses during a baseline assessment session of ADV. As teens progress through the program, they can transition between tracks as appropriate (e.g., a nondater who begins dating can transition to a dater track).

Across all tracks, key content on the warning signs of ADV, statistics on ADV, and expectations regarding the balance of power in dating relationships are covered. Modules cover assessment and feedback of stage of change for using healthy relationship skills and up to five stage-matched principles for using such skills. Additionally, assessment and feedback of alcohol use, its relationship to peer violence, and help seeking for oneself or peers are included.

Supplementary intervention components in an RCT trial of this program included a program website with personal homepage to replay session feedback, 15 videos demonstrating healthy relationship skills, school posters promoting the program, and a family guide providing basic ADV information and appropriate steps caregivers can take should their children report ADV.

Glass et al. (2022) developed an interactive safety-decision phone app, *myPlan*, for victimized college women and their friends. The creators are currently evaluating a version of this program suitable for younger adolescents as well. The myPlan app is free and accessible via a mobile app and a website (https://myPlanApp.org/). For safety, the app requires a self-created login PIN, as well as a "dummy" PIN should a dating partner force a user to unlock their phone. In this case, the "dummy" code merely unlocks a generic application about planning to stay organized.

The myPlan app aims to address three core components: protecting oneself by increasing safety behaviors, enhancing safe decision making, and reducing ADV. Within the app, users complete an assessment of their relationship health, safety priorities, and level of severity and risk for ADV in their current relationship. Based on this information, myPlan provides personalized safety planning information via a scoring algorithm that converts one's responses to easily understandable risk levels: (1) variable danger/low risk, (2) increased danger, (3) severe danger, and (4) extreme danger.

Within the intervention content, myPlan includes psychoeducation on relationship myths (e.g., jealousy equals love); characteristics of a healthy relationship; self-assessments with immediate feedback on red flags for an unhealthy relationship; a danger assessment and risk assessment for repeated acts of severe ADV; an interactive visual aid that allows users to make comparisons of the importance between priorities including privacy, feelings for dating partner, safety, well-being of children (as appropriate), academic success, and social support and status. Finally, the app also introduces each user to a safety plan with personalized strategies and referrals.

Couple Interventions

Although there is some controversy surrounding treatment of couples in which ADV or IPV is actively occurring, a brief motivational interviewing intervention for ADV among emerging adults shows some promise (Woodin & O'Leary 2010). Note that this intervention excludes any couples who report significant fear of their partner or serious physical injury; thus, it appears most appropriate for low to moderate levels of ADV. Following an assessment session including paper questionnaires of ADV and relationship satisfaction, as well as an oral history interview, couples receive a motivational feedback session.

Brief motivational interviewing for low-to-moderate ADV shows promise in reducing partner violence

Motivational sessions are individual (approximately 45 minutes each) and begin with feedback regarding participants' self-reported aggressive behaviors, aggression risk factors (e.g., alcohol use), and consequences of aggression (e.g., psychopathology, relationship distress). Motivational feedback shows participants how their reports compare with those of the average college student for each domain (i.e., behaviors, risk factors, consequences). This is followed by collaborative discussion of the impact of aggression on relationships and possible behavior change. Therapists reinforce change talk throughout the feedback session. Following the individual feedback sessions, couples reunite for a guided discussion of relationship hopes and concerns. For safety and confidentiality purposes, personalized feedback from the individual sessions is not referenced during the conjoint discussion.

Summary

There are many existing ADV programs available, and it can be tricky to know where to start in the selection process.

Clinicians should first identify as many of the following components as practically possible: *Who*, *What*, *Where*, *When*, and *How* do they seek to provide an intervention. By clarifying these components, clinicians can reference strong, empirically supported programs listed through section 4.2 of this book. Every program listed has been tested with real adolescents and emerging adults and found to have positive impacts on the lives of youths, and thus comes recommended by the authors when applied to appropriate audiences. We encourage clinicians to familiarize themselves with the program manuals and information for those interventions most fitting to their scope of practice. As illustrated in the Case Vignette at the conclusion of this book, multipronged interventions are likely beneficial (e.g., school-based as well as individual treatment approaches).

4.2.6 Addressing ADV in the Context of Other Treatment

Across interventions developed specifically for ADV, we see frequent reliance on social learning theory, feminist theory, and general group process, as well as elements drawn from CBT, motivational interviewing, and dialectical behavior therapy (DBT). As such, we encourage practitioners and intervention developers to familiarize themselves with foundational texts and practical elements in these areas. This is especially important given that there are several circumstances in which ADV perpetration or victimization arises in the context of treatment for another (related or unrelated) clinical issue. For instance, adolescents seeking psychological treatment for ongoing depressive symptoms may disclose experiences of relationship abuse or assault, express endorsement of maladaptive dating beliefs (e.g., rape myths), or report difficulty with conflict resolution in their romantic relationships.

Interventions like DBT (Linehan, 2014) and DBT-A (Rathus & Miller, 2015) may be helpful in addressing intense anger, emotional dysregulation, stormy relationships, and interpersonal (in)effectiveness present among ADV-impacted youths. However, it is important to note that there have been no clinical trials to date that have tested the efficacy of DBT or aggression replacement training techniques on reductions in ADV victimization or perpetration. Thus, clinicians should exercise caution and professional judgment when selecting the appropriate evidence-based treatment option for individual cases.

Reducing negative violent experiences may be supported and catalyzed by increases in prosocial, positive interpersonal experiences. Self-efficacy to engage in positive interpersonal relationship skills (or refrain from aggressive behaviors) may also generalize to positive nonromantic peer interactions. Theory suggests that cross-cutting programs designed to address aggression in general, rather than specific ADV behaviors, may target overlapping risk factors of poor social-emotional regulation, deviant behaviors, and exposure to family violence (Foshee, Dixon, et al., 2015). For example, Wolfe and colleagues (2012) demonstrated positive impacts of the Fourth R program on resistance to negative peer pressure and peer conflict resolution strategies among treatment participants at follow-up.

4.3 Variations and Combinations of Methods

Because ADV is a multilayered problem, it necessitates a multilayered response. Some of the programs reviewed in this chapter are built from ecological systems conceptualization, such that they seek to engage individual, family, school, and community levels. However, it is important to remember that no single program has provided consistently superior results.

Widespread systemic cultural change around how we conceptualize and respond to violence, data-driven approaches to lessen unfettered access to lethal weapons, and increased access and engagement with evidence-based mental health services are key to strengthening healthy relationships among youths. More research is needed on the effectiveness of school-based versus community- and health care–based interventions, as well as the benefits of integrating or stacking programming across these settings. A systemic approach to ADV prevention could emphasize rehearsal and retrieval of key concepts (e.g., sexual consent, recognition of conflict escalation) across multiple settings and limit overlap of more cursory subject matter. Moreover, comprehensive prevention

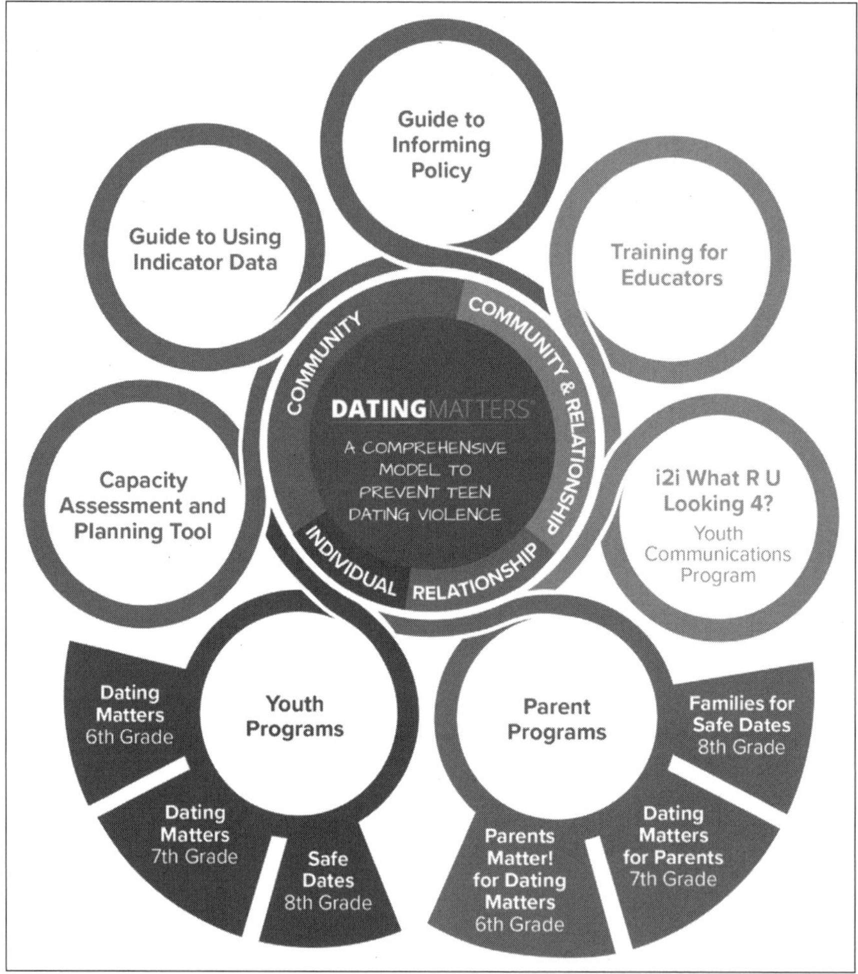

Figure 5

The seven components of the Dating Matters program. Reproduced from US Centers for Disease Control and Prevention (CDC) and available at https://vetoviolence.cdc.gov/ apps/dating-matters-toolkit/content/capacity-and-planning/ (Use of this material does not constitute endorsement of the authors by the U.S. Government, Department of Health and Human Services, or Centers for Disease Control and Prevention.)

approaches can address determinants of ADV at multiple levels of youths' social ecology across individual, peer, family, community, and societal systems.

One program that specifically addresses the multilayered nature of ADV is *Dating Matters*, a CDC-recognized comprehensive model that involves strategies for individual adolescents, peers, families, schools, and communities (Table 13, Box 3, and Table 14). The program is designed for 11- to 14-year-old early adolescents and aims to equip them with skills to reduce risky behaviors (e.g., substance use and sexual activities) and establish healthy relationships during or before the onset of dating. Dating Matters was designed initially for local health departments since these agencies tend to be community leaders with access to resources necessary for successful implementation.

As seen in Figure 5, Dating Matters comprises seven synergistic prevention components. Together, these components act to reinforce consistent and healthy relationship messages across contexts; promote complementary skills for youth, parents, and educators; and support these efforts through policy.

Table 13

Outline of the Different Components of the *Dating Matters* Program Used in School

Sixth grade	Seventh grade	Eighth grade
Youth programs		
Dating Matters program	Dating Matters program	Safe Dates program
Provides youth with opportunities to learn and enhance relationship skills in an engaging and nonthreatening manner, by first exploring what it means to have healthy friendships, across seven sessions.	Reinforces the information and skills developed in the sixth grade program, with seven sessions that provide further information on sexual violence, dating safety, and relationship rights, as well as access to supportive resources.	Builds upon the skills and knowledge students learn in the sixth- and seventh-grade Dating Matters programs, with 10 sessions focused more heavily on specific attitudes and behaviors related to teen dating violence, including sexual violence.
i2i: What R U Looking 4? youth communications program Reinforces messaging from the Dating Matters program for all grades, and promotes healthy dating behaviors by using teen-led communications strategies and messages to reach youths in their communities.		
Parent programs		
Parents Matter!	Dating Matters for Parents	Families for Safe Dates
Educates parents and caregivers through six group sessions on the issues their children face; improves their ability to communicate with their children about healthy relationships and sexuality; and helps them develop parenting practices that will decrease the likelihood of their children being exposed to unhealthy relationships.	Focuses on positive parenting and provides parents and caregivers with strategies and skills needed to communicate with their children about healthy relationships and sexual behaviors through three group sessions and three self-guided, in-home sessions.	Enables parents and their teens to jointly explore different topics regarding teen dating violence through five self-guided, in-home discussions.

Note. Adapted from https://vetoviolence.cdc.gov/apps/dating-matters-toolkit/content/get-started/

Box 3
Outline of the Different Components of the *Dating Matters* Program in Community Programs and Implementation Support

Dating Matters: Capacity Assessment and Planning Tool

Guides organizations in enhancing local public health capacity needed to implement comprehensive evidence-based and evidence-informed violence prevention strategies across their communities. It uses a collaborative four-step planning and action process developed by the CDC.

Dating Matters: Understanding teen dating violence prevention training for educators

Provides teachers and other school personnel with critical knowledge about teen dating violence as well as the specific skills, strategies, and resources needed to prevent violence from occurring and to implement prevention activities in their schools.

Dating Matters: Interactive guide to informing policy

Provides an overview of policy approaches to teen dating violence prevention, important considerations for informing policy, guidance for developing a policy plan, and tools and resources related to policy development, implementation, and evaluation.

Dating Matters guide to implementation

Guides LHDs, or other lead CBOs, in planning and successfully implementing the Dating Matters model and includes information on capacity building, staffing needs, building community. partnerships and engaging stakeholders, planning a budget, recruiting and engaging participants, tracking outcomes, and sustainability planning.

Coaches' playbook

Provides guidance for Dating Matters coaches in their role overseeing and supporting youth and parent program facilitators. The guidance includes information on characteristics of good facilitators, training, supervision, and monitoring fidelity.

Online facilitator trainings for youth and parent programs

Training for youth and parent program facilitators including interactive exercises, quizzes, video demonstrations featuring experienced youth and parent program facilitators, and homework assignments to reinforce skills and knowledge. The online site also includes an accompanying training manual.

Team Up! for Dating Matters community of practice

Online community of practice for everyone involved in implementing Dating Matters. Utilizes a free webbased or mobile application to create a virtual place for communities to collaborate, problem-solve, and share knowledge about Dating Matters implementation.

Note. Adapted from https://vetoviolence.cdc.gov/apps/dating-matters-toolkit/content/get-started/ CBO = Community Based Organization; CDC = Centers for Disease Control and Prevention; LHD = Local Health Department.

Table 14
Four Phases for Implementing the Dating Matters Model

Phase	Components
1: Understanding the dating matters model	• Learn about the development and goals of Dating Matters • Get familiar with all seven components of the model • Explore the Dating Matters Toolkit
2: Assessing capacity to implement dating matters and engage partners[a]	• Identify and engage partners and stakeholders • Complete the Dating Matters Capacity Assessment and Planning Tool • Develop a community advisory board

Table 14 Continued

Phase	Components
3: Preparing for implementation	• Create a logic model • Create an implementation action plan • Plan for your budget and staffing • Develop a recruitment plan for schools and parents • Adapt program materials (as needed) • Join the Team Up! for Dating Matters community of practice to learn from others and share your progress
4: Planning for evaluation and sustainability	• Plan for program monitoring and evaluation • Implement policy and indicators components of Dating Matters • Plan for sustainability

Note. Adapted from https://vetoviolence.cdc.gov/apps/dating-matters-toolkit/content/get-started/ CDC = Centers for Disease Control and Prevention. [a]Also known as the General Capacity Assessment and Planning Tool.

All tools, resources, and planning materials for implementing the comprehensive Dating Matters model are available online at no cost (https://vetoviolence.cdc.gov/apps/dating-matters-toolkit/content/get-started). Multiple evaluations of the Dating Matters model show promising results on ADV perpetration, victimization, and relationship behaviors (DeGue et al., 2021; Niolon et al., 2019).

4.4 Problems in Carrying Out the Interventions

4.4.1 Practical Barriers

Implementing ADV interventions, particularly with any sort of treatment fidelity, involves several challenges. Among these, money and time are two particularly consistent and resounding barriers reported by patients and communities at large. Existing ADV programs differ widely in length, both in number of sessions and duration of each session.

Note that among the programs reviewed in the prior section, length ranged from a single session to 3 years of programming. Theoretically, longer interventions may grant increased opportunity to present and rehearse information or behavioral skills (i.e., the larger the dose, the better the response). Longer interventions may also be able to cover a greater breadth of ADV content or provide more repetition of important material. Yet, time-consuming programs may be unattractive to adolescents, resulting in greater attrition or reduced engagement. Lengthy programs may be similarly unattractive, due to potential cost and time taken from academic instruction or facility budgets. At facilities where youth or provider turnover is high, youths may not receive all intended content of a lengthy intervention. This last point is especially problematic when material builds upon content presented during previous lessons.

We also see that those at heightened risk for ADV due to factors such as justice involvement, poverty, and homelessness, are the same youths facing chronic absenteeism from school, lack of consistent medical care, and fewer opportunities to pursue higher education. These disadvantages render our most vulnerable, highest-risk youths as substantially less likely to *ever* be exposed to existing ADV programs, which are commonly delivered in schools, medical facilities, and colleges.

4.4.2 Contraindications

Addressing ADV may be contraindicated with adolescents and emerging adults who are in actively violent relationships. Particularly within the adult IPV literature, there is spirited debate about providing couples therapy to address the abuse when one or both partners are not ready or willing to leave the relationship. Arguments against treating ADV under these circumstances include:

- Attendance in couples counseling can inadvertently imply that ADV is a mutual relationship problem, which may justify the violence, or lead to inappropriately blaming victims for their victimization.
- Reaching mutual agreement on treatment goals is difficult (if not impossible) when relationship power dynamics are abusive. Shared treatment goals necessitate some level of egalitarian power distribution, which is absent when one dating partner seeks to control the other through violence, threats of violence, or psychological abuse.
- A perpetrator may use therapy and its tools (e.g., compromise, emotional monitoring) to further control their dating partner.
- Individuals are less likely to feel safe, speak up, or share openly in the presence of an abuser. This directly negates several hallmarks of effective psychotherapy – namely, safety, vulnerability, and open communication.

However, some interventions show efficacy even in actively violent contexts. That said, adolescent relationships are known to be relatively brief, and marked by lower levels of emotionally intimacy and commitment compared with monogamous adult partnerships. Thus, couples-based treatment approaches are unlikely to be the most suitable or appropriate options until emerging adulthood or beyond (not to mention difficulties with consent and mandated reporting when working with clients who are minors). As stated in section 4.2, interventions focused on individual victims or perpetrators are also available (see Interventions Designed for Perpetrators and Interventions Designed for Victims), and many provide resources and tools to evaluate, modify, and safely exit an abusive relationship.

4.5   Multicultural Considerations

Across all populations, openly discussing beliefs and values is imperative. Early on in treatment, assessing important family and cultural beliefs can also encourage engagement and joining in, and enhance the therapeutic alliance. Discussing ADV brings up a plethora of sensitive topics, with vast cultural differences in how one is expected to appropriately navigate such conversations. These topics can include discussions of violence, sexual behavior, injury and infection, pregnancy and contraception, dating habits, sexuality and sexual orientation, gender expression, parental monitoring, spirituality and religion, gender roles, degree of family involvement, substance use and risky behavior, and even outcries of traumatic or abusive experiences in other relationships. No two adolescents will share the same degree of comfort, the same values, or the same opinions on these matters.

To build engagement, early treatment should assess family and cultural beliefs around sensitive topics like ADV

4.5.1   Race and Ethnicity

While addressing ADV, it is essential to consider the unique experiences, cultural contexts, and potential barriers that individuals from different backgrounds may face, including:

1. **Cultural sensitivity:** Understand that cultural values, norms, and expectations can vary across races and ethnicities. It is crucial to approach treatment with cultural sensitivity and respect for diverse perspectives. Consider the impact of cultural factors such as family dynamics, gender roles, and community support systems.
2. **Language and communication:** Language barriers can impede effective communication and hinder treatment efforts. Providing interpreters or bilingual staff can help ensure individuals from diverse backgrounds can express themselves and feel welcomed.
3. **Community engagement:** Engaging with community organizations and leaders who are trusted within specific racial or ethnic communities can help create culturally competent support networks. These organizations can provide resources, raise awareness, and offer guidance on addressing ADV within their respective communities.
4. **Tailored interventions:** Recognize that different populations may have distinct needs and preferences when it comes to interventions. It may be necessary to adapt therapeutic approaches, considering factors such as cultural values, belief systems, and historical trauma. Collaborating with individuals from diverse racial backgrounds can help develop strategies that are effective and culturally appropriate.
5. **Trauma-informed care:** Many individuals who experience ADV may also have experienced trauma. It is crucial to provide trauma-informed care that acknowledges and addresses the potential impact of historical, intergenerational, or race-related trauma. Understanding these factors can help shape treatment plans that promote healing and resilience.

6. **Intersectionality:** Recognize that individuals may experience overlapping forms of oppression and discrimination due to their race, gender, sexual orientation, or other identities. Intersectionality acknowledges the interconnectedness of these factors and the unique challenges faced by individuals with multiple marginalized identities. Incorporating an intersectional lens when treating ADV can help provide more comprehensive and effective support.

7. **Prevention and education:** Promote prevention efforts and educational programs that are inclusive and accessible to individuals from all racial backgrounds. This can involve teaching healthy relationship skills, raising awareness about ADV, and providing resources to empower individuals to recognize and address unhealthy behaviors early on.

4.5.2   LGBTQIA+

Treating ADV in lesbian, gay, bisexual, transgender, queer/questioning, intersex, asexual, and other (LGBTQIA+) adolescents requires a comprehensive and sensitive approach that takes into account the unique experiences and challenges faced by this population.

1. **Create a safe and supportive environment:** Provide a safe and inclusive space where LGBTQIA+ adolescents feel comfortable in openly expressing their experiences, which includes an environment free of judgment and discrimination.

2. **Raise awareness and education:** Educate both LGBTQIA+ adolescents and professionals working with them about healthy relationships, consent, and the different forms of ADV.

3. **Address intersectional experiences:** Recognize that LGBTQIA+ adolescents may face additional challenges related to their intersecting identities, such as racism, ableism, or religious discrimination. An intersectional approach acknowledges and addresses these unique experiences in the context of ADV.

4. **Tailor interventions to LGBTQIA+ needs:** Develop interventions and resources specifically designed for LGBTQ+ adolescents, considering their specific experiences and barriers. This may include addressing issues like outing threats, internalized homophobia or transphobia, and lack of support from family or peers.

5. **Collaborate with LGBTQIA+-affirming organizations:** Partner with organizations and professionals who can provide specialized support, guidance, and resources for both prevention and intervention efforts.

6. **Supportive counseling and therapy:** Encourage LGBTQIA+ adolescents who have experienced ADV to seek professional counseling or therapy. Mental health professionals who are knowledgeable about LGBTQIA+ issues can provide a safe space for discussing trauma, exploring coping strategies, and building resilience.

7. **Foster peer support networks:** Encourage the formation of LGBTQIA+ support groups or safe spaces where adolescents can connect with peers who have had similar experiences.

4.5.3   Adolescents With Disabilities

Preventing and treating relationship abuse in adolescents with disabilities requires a thoughtful and comprehensive approach that considers their specific needs and challenges. While all adolescents, regardless of disability status, need to learn the same essential information about relationships (e.g., characteristics of healthy relationships, consent, communication, recognizing signs of abuse), adaptations to how the information is taught may be needed.

Specifically, the information should be provided in accessible formats, using appropriate communication methods for each individual's unique abilities, strengths, and challenges. This latter point may include personalized support and accommodations, such as *augmentative and alternative communication* (AAC) device aid, simplified language, other assistive technology, neurodiversity-embracing social communication training, or additional counseling or therapy sessions.

The content of dating violence treatment and prevention approaches should also be reviewed for ableism or content that is insensitive to the diverse lived experiences of youths with disabilities. For example, not all youths with disabilities have friends, so curricula that assume youths have friends can worsen feelings of isolation. Further, prevention programs – whether individual-, school-, or community-based – should be adapted to ensure accessibility, both in terms of content and delivery methods. Perhaps most importantly, providers should adopt a multidisciplinary approach to address ADV in children with disabilities and work collaboratively with professionals from various fields to ensure a comprehensive assessment, intervention, and support plan that considers all aspects of the adolescent's well-being.

Remember that every individual's experience is unique, and it is important to approach each situation with empathy, respect, and cultural humility. By providing support, education, and inclusive resources, we can help all adolescents affected by ADV to heal, build healthy relationships, and thrive.

5

Case Vignette

Treating Adolescent Relationship Abuse

This case vignette is a fictional scenario created to illustrate the process of treating adolescent relationship abuse. It is important to note that each case is unique, and the treatment approach may vary based on individual and school circumstances.

Client Information

Sarah is a 16-year-old female high school student in her junior year at Roosevelt High School. She lives with her parents and two younger siblings. Sarah is academically gifted and involved in extracurricular activities. She recently started dating Alex, a 17-year-old junior from her school. Over the past few months, Sarah's friends and family have noticed changes in her behavior and demeanor.

Presenting Concern

Sarah's close friend, Emma, approached the school counselor, expressing concerns about Sarah's well-being. Emma noticed that Sarah has become increasingly withdrawn and anxious, often making excuses to avoid social events. She also witnessed an incident where Sarah and Alex had a heated argument during school lunch, with Alex raising his voice and displaying aggressive behavior.

Initial Assessment

The school counselor, Ms. Johnson, scheduled a meeting with Sarah to discuss her concerns. During the meeting, Sarah appeared nervous and avoided eye contact. Ms. Johnson created a safe and nonjudgmental environment for Sarah to share her experiences. Through gentle probing and open-ended questions, she discovered the following:

1. **Pattern of abuse:** Sarah revealed that Alex frequently insults her, belittles her achievements, and isolates her from friends and family. He often controls her activities and constantly checks her phone and social media

accounts. Sarah expressed feeling scared, trapped, and unable to break free from the relationship.

2. **Emotional impact:** Sarah shared that she has been feeling anxious, depressed, and constantly on edge. She described experiencing a loss of self-esteem and a decline in her academic performance. She admitted that she had been afraid to speak up about the abuse due to fear of retaliation or losing Alex's affection.

3. **Isolation:** Sarah revealed that Alex discourages her from spending time with friends and often creates conflicts when she attempts to maintain those relationships. Consequently, Sarah's social circle has significantly diminished, leaving her feeling alone and isolated.

Intervention Plan

Given the severity of the situation, Ms. Johnson determines that Sarah needs a comprehensive plan to address the abuse. She collaborates with Sarah and her parents (after receiving Sarah's permission to contact them) to establish the following goals:

1. **Safety planning:** Ensuring Sarah's immediate safety is of utmost importance. Develop a safety plan with the client to ensure her physical and emotional well-being. Identify trusted adults, such as school staff or family members, whom she can reach out to in case of emergencies or when she needs support.

2. **Psychoeducation:** Ms. Johnson provides Sarah with information about healthy relationships and the dynamics of abusive relationships. Sarah learns to identify red flags and warning signs of abusive behavior, empowering her to recognize and respond to similar situations in the future.

3. **Individual counseling:** Ms. Johnson recommends Sarah begin individual counseling sessions with a qualified mental health professional in the community. The focus is on rebuilding her self-esteem, addressing her trauma symptoms, and developing coping strategies for managing anxiety and depression. Ms. Johnson recommends finding providers trained in evidence-based therapeutic modalities including cognitive behavior therapy and trauma-focused therapy.

4. **Supportive services:** Ms. Johnson connects Sarah and her parents with external resources, including local domestic violence shelters, hotlines, and support groups. These services provide additional support and guidance to both Sarah and her family throughout the healing process.

5. **School involvement:** Ms. Johnson liaises with Sarah's teachers and school administration to ensure they are aware of the situation. Together, they implement safety measures at school, such as adjusting class schedules and providing increased supervision during breaks.

6. **Family therapy:** Recognizing the importance of family support, Ms. Johnson recommends engaging in family therapy sessions with a qualified community mental health provider. These sessions aim to enhance com-

munication, strengthen the support system, and facilitate healing within the family unit.

Client Follow-Up

Over time, Sarah's self-esteem improves, and she develops assertiveness skills to set boundaries in her relationships. She actively participates in support groups and engages with other survivors of relationship abuse. The collaborative effort between Sarah, her family, her community therapist, and the school counselor aids in recovery from the traumatic experience.

School Follow-Up

Roosevelt High School, where Sarah attends, is a large public high school located in a suburban community. The school serves a diverse student population, with approximately 1,500 students ranging in age from 13 to 19 years. In recent years and in addition to Sarah's case, there have been instances of unhealthy relationships among students, including incidents of dating violence, emotional abuse, and toxic behavior. Concerned about these issues, the school administration decides to implement a comprehensive healthy relationship program to promote respectful and positive interactions among students.

To address the growing concern over unhealthy relationships, the school administration appoints a team of staff members, including Ms. Johnson (school counselor), a health education teacher, and a social worker, to spearhead the implementation of a healthy relationship program. To determine next steps, the team collaborates with a local university and community organizations that specialize in ADV and relationship education.

They first decide to conduct a thorough needs assessment to gain insights into the existing knowledge and attitudes of the student body regarding healthy relationships. They administer anonymous surveys, conduct focus groups, and hold individual interviews with students, teachers, and parents to gather information. The data collected highlights a lack of awareness about healthy relationship dynamics, consent, communication skills, and identifying warning signs of abusive behavior.

Based on the needs assessment, the team decides they need to identify and implement a curriculum that includes various components, such as:

1. **Information on healthy relationships:** Students learn about the characteristics of healthy relationships, including trust, respect, communication, and consent. They explore different relationship types, such as friendships, romantic relationships, and familial relationships.
2. **Communication skills:** Students develop effective communication skills, including active listening, assertiveness, and conflict resolution techniques. Students engage in role-plays and group discussions to practice these skills in realistic scenarios.

3. **Consent and boundaries:** Students learn about the importance of consent in all types of relationships and behaviors. Students understand the concept of consent and explore scenarios to determine what constitutes consensual and nonconsensual behavior. Discussions on personal boundaries and how to establish and respect them are also included.
4. **Recognizing and responding to unhealthy relationships:** Students are taught to identify warning signs of unhealthy relationships, such as controlling behavior, manipulation, and verbal or physical abuse. They learn how to seek help for themselves or others who may be in abusive situations and the available support resources both inside and outside the school.

In talking with school personnel and students, it was clear that substance use and risky sexual behavior were co-occurring problems with unhealthy relationships. Thus, rather than taking a piecemeal approach, the administrative team looked to identify a program that targeted multiple problem behaviors. Further, school leadership informed the administrative team that they had a limited budget and little available time, so the program had to be affordable and feasible. Weighing these options, the administrative team settled on the Fourth R program, as it has been shown to be effective, is facilitated by existing teachers, and met the health curriculum standards set forth be the state and federal government.

Implementation and Evaluation

The school partnered with faculty at the local university to ensure that the program is delivered with fidelity. Throughout the program, the team regularly assesses the effectiveness of the program through anonymous student surveys, teacher feedback, and observation. They noted positive changes in student attitudes, improved communication skills, increased awareness of warning signs, and a willingness to seek help when needed.

In addition to evaluating the immediate impact of the program, the team tracked long-term outcomes by monitoring incidents of unhealthy relationships and the utilization of support services over the following academic years. This information was used to make adjustments to the program and ensure its continued effectiveness.

Conclusion

Through the implementation of a comprehensive healthy relationship program, Roosevelt High School aims to equip its students with the knowledge and skills necessary to foster respectful and positive relationships. By promoting open communication, consent, and the identification of warning signs, the program aims to create a safer and more supportive environment for all students, ultimately helping them develop healthy relationships that positively impact their lives beyond high school.

6

Further Reading and Resources

Books

Devaney, J., Bradbury-Jones, C., Macy, R. J., Øverlien, C., & Holt, S. (Eds.). (2021). *The Routledge international handbook of domestic violence and abuse*. Routledge. https://doi.org/10.4324/9780429331053
This edited book provides a comprehensive and multidisciplinary overview of the causes, consequences, and patterns of domestic violence, which offers a theoretical and empirical foundation that can be applied to adolescent dating contexts.

Wolfe, D., & Temple, J. R. (Eds.). (2018). *Adolescent dating violence: Theory, research, and prevention*. Academic Press.
This edited book provides a detailed overview and theoretical underpinnings of how dating violence develops in adolescence, including risk and protective factors.

Journals

The following journals routinely provide peer-reviewed empirical work related to ADV, IPV, and clinical treatment of aggression and victimization among adolescents:

JAMA Pediatrics; Journal of Adolescent Health; Journal of Clinical Child & Adolescent Psychology; Journal of Interpersonal Violence; Journal of Research on Adolescence; Journal of School Violence; Journal of Youth & Adolescence; Prevention Science; Psychology of Violence; Trauma, Violence, & Abuse.

Crisis Services

The National Domestic Violence Hotline

1-800-799-SAFE or text START to 88788
https://www.thehotline.org/

A nonprofit hotline and organization established in 1996 from the Violence Against Women Act. Services include crisis intervention, information, and referrals for victims and perpetrators of ADV/IPV, as well as their friends and families. The hotline is toll-free, confidential, and anonymous.

The National Dating Abuse Helpline

1-866-331-9474 or text LOVEIS to 22522
https://Loveisrespect.org

A 24-hour hotline, text-line, and webpage resource designed specifically for teens and young adults. One-on-one support from peer advocates is offered in real-time.

Websites

Love is respect

https://www.loveisrespect.org/search-our-resources/

In this helpful page you can search for a wide range of resources, including on healthy relationships, personal safety, consent, boundaries, and warning signs of abuse. You can search by keyword or through popular featured entries like "How to fight fair" and "What consent does – and doesn't – look like." It also prominently encourages safety online by offering a quick-exit feature and tips for protecting your privacy if your browsing might be monitored.

Jennifer Ann's Group

https://jenniferann.org/

This page includes general information about dating violence, including awareness, education, and advocacy resources.

National Sexual Violence Resource Center

https://www.nsvrc.org/blogs/teen-dating-violence-prevention-resources-2025-update

Compilation of resources, including toolkits, social media guides, and printable materials (e.g., consent-themed valentines, chatterboxes, coloring pages), as well as informative reports and manuals for advocates, caregivers, and parents.

National Domestic Violence Hotline

https://www.thehotline.org

This is a comprehensive, free, and confidential resource offering 24/7 live support, including phone, chat, and text, as well as comprehensive educational materials on relationship abuse, safety planning tools, culturally specific services, and resources for survivors, allies, and those causing harm.

7

References

Adhia, A., Kernic, M. A., Hemenway, D., Vavilala, M. S., & Rivara, F. P. (2019). Intimate partner homicide of adolescents. *JAMA Pediatrics, 173*(6), 571–577. https://doi.org/10.1001/jamapediatrics.2019.0621

American Psychiatric Association. (2022). *Diagnostic and statistical manual of mental disorders* (5th ed., text rev.). https://doi.org/10.1176/appi.books.9780890425787

Arriaga, X. B., & Foshee, V. A. (2004). Adolescent dating violence: Do adolescents follow in their friends' or their parents' footsteps? *Journal of Interpersonal Violence, 19*(2), 162–184. https://doi.org/10.1177/0886260503260247

Baiden, P., Mengo, C., & Small, E. (2021). History of physical teen dating violence and its association with suicidal behaviors among adolescent high school students: Results from the 2015 Youth Risk Behavior Survey. *Journal of Interpersonal Violence, 36*(17–18), NP9526–NP9547. https://doi.org/10.1177/0886260519860087

Baker, C. K., Naai, R., Mitchell, J., & Trecker, C. (2014). Utilizing a train-the-trainer model for sexual violence prevention: Findings from a pilot study with high school students of Asian and Pacific Islander descent in Hawai'i. *Asian American Journal of Psychology, 5*(2), 106–115. https://doi.org/10.1037/a0034670

Ball, B., Tharp, A. T., Noonan, R. K., Valle, L. A., Hamburger, M. E., & Rosenbluth, B. (2012). Expect respect support groups: preliminary evaluation of a dating violence prevention program for at-risk youth. *Violence Against Women, 18*(7), 746–762. https://doi.org/10.1177/1077801212455188

Basile, K. C., Clayton, H. B., DeGue, S., Gilford, J. W., Vagi, K. J., Suarez, N. A., Zwald, M. L., & Lowry, R. (2020). Interpersonal violence victimization among high school students – Youth Risk Behavior Survey, United States, 2019. *Morbidity and Mortality Weekly Report (MMWR), 69*(1), 28–37. https//doi.org/10.15585/mmwr.su6901a4

Bell, K. M., & Naugle, A. E. (2008). Intimate partner violence theoretical considerations: Moving towards a contextual framework. *Clinical Psychology Review, 28*(7), 1096–1107. https://doi.org/10.1016/j.cpr.2008.03.003

Bender, A. K., Koegler, E., Johnson, S. D., Murugan, V., & Wamser-Nanney, R. (2021). Guns and intimate partner violence among adolescents: A scoping review. *Journal of Family Violence, 36*, 605–617. https://doi.org/10.1007/s10896-020-00193-x

Benson, M. L., Wooldredge, J., Thistlethwaite, A. B., & Fox, G. L. (2004). The correlation between race and domestic violence is confounded with community context. *Social Problems, 51*(3), 326–342. https://doi.org/10.1525/sp.2004.51.3.326

Briere, J. (1996). Trauma symptom checklist for children. *Psychological Assessment Resources*, 00253-8.

Carver, K., Joyner, K., & Udry J. R. (2003). National estimates of adolescent romantic relationships. In P. Florsheim (Ed.), *Adolescent romantic relations and sexual behavior: Theory, research, and practical implications* (pp. 23–56). Psychology Press. https://doi.org/10.4324/9781410607782

Centers for Disease Control and Prevention. (2021). *1991–2021 High School Youth Risk Behavior Survey data*. https://nccd.cdc.gov/youthonline/.

Centers for Disease Control and Prevention. (2022). *Preventing intimate partner violence: Fact Sheet*. https://www.cdc.gov/intimate-partner-violence/prevention/index.html

Cheung, W. W., Caduff, A., & Raj, A. (2023). The association between dating violence and student absenteeism among a representative sample of US high school students: Findings from the 2019 Youth Risk Behavior Survey. *Journal of Interpersonal Violence, 38*(1-2), 2218–2233. https://doi.org/10.1177/08862605221090564

Choi, H. J., Elmquist, J., Shorey, R. C., Rothman, E. F., Stuart, G. L., & Temple, J. R. (2017). Stability of alcohol use and teen dating violence for female youth: A latent transition analysis. *Drug and Alcohol Review, 36*(1), 80–87. https://doi.org/10.1111/dar.12462

Cloitre, M., Stolbach, B. C., Herman, J. L., Kolk, B. V. D., Pynoos, R., Wang, J., & Petkova, E. (2009). A developmental approach to complex PTSD: Childhood and adult cumulative trauma as predictors of symptom complexity. *Journal of Traumatic Stress, 22*(5), 399–408. https://doi.org/10.1002/jts.20444

Cohen, J. A., Mannarino, A. P., & Deblinger, E. (Eds.). (2012). *Trauma-focused CBT for children and adolescents: Treatment applications.* Guilford Press.

Cohen, J. R., Shorey, R. C., Menon, S. V., & Temple, J. R. (2018). Predicting teen dating violence perpetration. *Pediatrics, 141*(4), e20172790. https://doi.org/10.1542/peds.2017-2790

Coker, A. L., Bush, H. M., Clear, E. R., Brancato, C. J., & McCauley, H. L. (2020). Bystander program effectiveness to reduce violence and violence acceptance within sexual minority male and female high school students using a cluster RCT. *Prevention Science, 21*, 434–444. https://doi.org/10.1007/s11121-019-01073-7

Collibee, C., Fox, K., Folk, J., Rizzo, C., Kemp, K., & Tolou-Shams, M. (2022). Dating aggression among court-involved adolescents: prevalence, offense type, and gender. *Journal of Interpersonal Violence, 37*(13-14), NP12695–NP12705. https://doi.org/10.1177/0886260521997955

Congressional Research Service. (1993, September 10). Violence Against Women Act of 1993: S. 11, 103rd Cong. ProQuest Congressional.

Crane, C. A., & Eckhardt, C. I. (2013). Negative affect, alcohol consumption, and female-to-male intimate partner violence: A daily diary investigation. *Partner Abuse, 4*, 332–355. https://doi.org/10.1891/1946-6560.4.3.332

Cunningham, R. M., Walton, M. A., Goldstein, A., Chermack, S. T., Shope, J. T., Raymond Bingham, C., & Blow, F. C. (2009). Three-month follow-up of brief computerized and therapist interventions for alcohol and violence among teens. *Academic Emergency Medicine, 16*(11), 1193–1207. https://doi.org/10.1111/j.1553-2712.2009.00513.x

Davidson, M. M. (2005). *Adolescent attitudes regarding dating relationships: The construction of sex-specific scales* [Unpublished doctoral dissertation]. Columbia, MO: University of Missouri-Columbia.

DeGue, S., Niolon, P. H., Estefan, L. F., Tracy, A. J., Le, V. D., Vivolo-Kantor, A. M., Little, T. D., Latzman, N. E., Tharp, A., Lang, K. M., Taylor, B. (2021). Effects of Dating Matters® on sexual violence and sexual harassment outcomes among middle school youth: A cluster-randomized controlled trial. *Prevention Science, 22*(2), 175–185.

De La Rue, L., Polanin, J. R., Espelage, D. L., & Pigott, T. D. (2017). A meta-analysis of school-based interventions aimed to prevent or reduce violence in teen dating relationships. *Review of Educational Research, 87*(1), 7–34. https://doi.org/10.3102/0034654316632061

DePrince, A. P., Chu, A. T., Labus, J., Shirk, S. R., & Potter, C. (2015). Testing two approaches to revictimization prevention among adolescent girls in the child welfare system. *Journal of Adolescent Health, 56*(2), S33–S39. https://doi.org/10.1016/j.jadohealth.2014.06.022

Dishion, T. J., McCord, J., & Poulin, F. (1999). When interventions harm: Peer groups and problem behavior. *American Psychologist, 54*(9), 755–764. https://doi.org/10.1037/0003-066X.54.9.755

Dobash, R. E., & Dobash, R. (1979). *Violence against wives: A case against the patriarchy* (Vol. 15). Free Press.

Exner-Cortens, D., Eckenrode, J., Bunge, J., & Rothman, E. (2017). Revictimization after adolescent dating violence in a matched, national sample of youth. *Journal of Adolescent Health, 60*(2), 176–183. https://doi.org/10.1016/j.jadohealth.2016.09.015

Exner-Cortens, D., Eckenrode, J., & Rothman, E. (2013). Longitudinal associations between teen dating violence victimization and adverse health outcomes. *Pediatrics, 131*(1), 71–78. https://doi.org/10.1542/peds.2012-1029

Fernández-González, L., Calvete, E., & Orue, I. (2020). Adolescent dating violence stability and mutuality: A 4-year longitudinal study. *Journal of Interpersonal Violence, 35*(9-10), 2012–2032. https://doi.org/10.1177/0886260517699953

Finkelhor, D., Vanderminden, J., Turner, H., Shattuck, A., & Hamby, S. (2014). Youth exposure to violence prevention programs in a national sample. *Child Abuse & Neglect, 38*(4), 677–686. https://doi.org/10.1016/j.chiabu.2014.01.010

Firestone, R. W., & Firestone, L. A. (2008). *Firestone Assessment of Violent Thoughts-Adolescent: FAVT-A; Professional manual.* Psychological Assessment Resources.

Foshee, V. A., Bauman, K. E., Arriaga, X. B., Helms, R. W., Koch, G. G., & Linder, G. F. (1998). An evaluation of Safe Dates, an adolescent dating violence prevention program. *American Journal of Public Health, 88,* 45–50. https://doi.org/10.2105/AJPH.88.1.45

Foshee, V. A., Benefield, T., Dixon, K. S., Chang, L. Y., Senkomago, V., Ennett, S. T., Moracco, K. E., & Bowling, J. M. (2015). The effects of Moms and Teens for Safe Dates: A dating abuse prevention program for adolescents exposed to domestic violence. *Journal of Youth and Adolescence, 44*(5), 995–1010. https://doi.org/10.1007/s10964-015-0272-6

Foshee, V. A., Dixon, K. S., Ennett, S. T., Moracco, K. E., Bowling, J. M., Chang, L.-Y., & Moss, J. L. (2015). The process of adapting a universal dating abuse prevention program to adolescents exposed to domestic violence. *Journal of Interpersonal Violence, 30*(12), 2151–2173. https://doi.org/10.1177/0886260514552278

Foshee, V. A., Linder, G. F., Bauman, K. E., Langwick, S. A., Arriaga, X. B., Heath, J. L., McMahon, P. M., & Bangdiwala, S. (1996). The Safe Dates Project: Theoretical basis, evaluation design, and selected baseline findings. *American Journal of Preventive Medicine, 12*(5), 39–47. https://doi.org/10.1016/S0749-3797(18)30235-6

Foshee, V. A., Reyes, H. L. M., Ennett, S. T., Cance, J. D., Bauman, K. E., & Bowling, J. M. (2012). Assessing the effects of Families for Safe Dates, a family-based teen dating abuse prevention program. *Journal of Adolescent Health, 51*(4), 349–356. https://doi.org/10.1016/j.jadohealth.2011.12.029

Gardner, S. P., & Boellaard, R. (2007). Does youth relationship education continue to work after a high school class? A longitudinal study. *Family Relations, 56*(5), 490–500. https://doi.org/10.1111/j.1741-3729.2007.00476.x

Gardner, S. P., Giese, K., & Parrott, S. M. (2004). Evaluation of the connections: Relationships and marriage curriculum. *Family Relations, 53*(5), 521–527. https://doi.org/10.1111/j.0197-6664.2004.00061.x

Gillum, T. L., & DiFulvio, G. (2012). "There's So Much at Stake" sexual minority youth discuss dating violence. *Violence Against Women, 18*(7), 725–745. https://doi.org/10.1177/1077801212455164

Giordano, P. C., Soto, D. A., Manning, W. D., & Longmore, M. A. (2010). The characteristics of romantic relationships associated with teen dating violence. *Social Science Research, 39*(6), 863–874. https://doi.org/10.1016/j.ssresearch.2010.03.009

Glass, N. E., Clough, A., Messing, J. T., Bloom, T., Brown, M. L., Eden, K. B., Campbell, J. C., Gielen, A., Laughon, K., Grace, K. T., Turner, R. M., Alvarez, C., Case, J., Barnes-Hoyt, J., Alhusen, J., Hanson, G. C., Perrin, N. A. (2022). Longitudinal impact of the myPlan app on health and safety among college women experiencing partner violence. *Journal of Interpersonal Violence, 37*(13-14), NP11436–NP11459. https://doi.org/10.1177/0886260521991880

Gonzalez-Guarda, R. M., Guerra, J. E., Cummings, A. A., Pino, K., & Becerra, M. M. (2015). Examining the preliminary efficacy of a dating violence prevention program for Hispanic adolescents. *Journal of School Nursing, 31*(6), 411–421. https://doi.org/10.1177/1059840515598843

Halpern, C. T., Oslak, S. G., Young, M. L., Martin, S. L., & Kupper, L. L. (2001). Partner violence among adolescents in opposite-sex romantic relationships: Findings from the National Longitudinal Study of Adolescent Health. *American Journal of Public Health, 91*(10), 1679–1685. https://doi.org/10.2105/AJPH.91.10.1679

Hamby, S. (2017). On defining violence, and why it matters [Editorial]. *Psychology of Violence, 7*(2), 167–180. https://doi.org/10.1037/vio0000117

Hatkevich, C., Mellick, W., Reuter, T., Temple, J. R., & Sharp, C. (2020). Dating violence victimization, nonsuicidal self-injury, and the moderating effect of borderline personality disorder features in adolescent inpatients. *Journal of Interpersonal Violence, 35*(15-16), 3124–3147. https://doi.org/10.1177/0886260517708402

Heyman, R. E., Slep, A. M. S., & Foran, H. M. (2015). Enhanced definitions of intimate partner violence for DSM-5 and ICD-11 may promote improved screening and treatment. *Family Process, 54*(1), 64–81. https://doi.org/10.1111/famp.12121

Hoefer, R., Black, B., & Ricard, M. (2015). The impact of state policy on teen dating violence prevalence. *Journal of Adolescence, 44*, 88–96. https://doi.org/10.1016/j.adolescence.2015.07.006

Huesmann, L. R., & Guerra, N. G. (1997). Children's normative beliefs about aggression and aggressive behavior. *Journal of Personality and Social Psychology, 72*(2), 408. https://doi.org/10.1037/0022-3514.72.2.408

Jaycox, L. H., McCaffrey, D., Eiseman, B., Aronoff, J., Shelley, G. A., Collins, R. L., & Marshall, G. N. (2006). Impact of a school-based dating violence prevention program among Latino teens: Randomized controlled effectiveness trial. *Journal of Adolescent Health, 39*(5), 694–704. https://doi.org/10.1016/j.jadohealth.2006.05.002

Johnson, W. L., Giordano, P. C., Manning, W. D., & Longmore, M. A. (2015). The age-IPV curve: Changes in the perpetration of intimate partner violence during adolescence and young adulthood. *Journal of Youth and Adolescence, 44*, 708–726. https://doi.org/10.1007/s10964-014-0158-z

Joppa, M. C., Rizzo, C. J., Nieves, A. V., & Brown, L. K. (2016). Pilot investigation of the Katie Brown educational program: A school-community partnership. *Journal of School Health, 86*(4), 288–297. https://doi.org/10.1111/josh.12378

Jouriles, E. N., Choi, H. J., Rancher, C., & Temple, J. R. (2017). Teen dating violence victimization, trauma symptoms, and revictimization in early adulthood. *Journal of Adolescent Health, 61*(1), 115–119. https://doi.org/10.1016/j.jadohealth.2017.01.020

Jouriles, E. N., Krauss, A., Vu, N. L., Banyard, V. L., & McDonald, R. (2018). Bystander programs addressing sexual violence on college campuses: A systematic review and meta-analysis of program outcomes and delivery methods. *Journal of American College Health, 66*(6), 457–466. https://doi.org/10.1080/07448481.2018.1431906

Jouriles, E. N., McDonald, R., Rosenfield, D., Levy, N., Sargent, K., Caiozzo, C., & Grych, J. H. (2016). TakeCARE, a video bystander program to help prevent sexual violence on college campuses: Results of two randomized, controlled trials. *Psychology of Violence, 6*(3), 410. https://doi.org/10.1037/vio0000016

Jouriles, E. N., Mueller, V., Rosenfield, D., McDonald, R., & Dodson, M. C. (2012). Teens' experiences of harsh parenting and exposure to severe intimate partner violence: Adding insult to injury in predicting teen dating violence. *Psychology of Violence, 2*(2), 125. https://doi.org/10.1037/a0027264

Kaplow, J. B., Rolon-Arroyo, B., Layne, C. M., Oosterhoff, B., Hill, R., Steinberg, A. M., & Pynoos, R. S. (2020). Validation of the UCLA PTSD Reaction Index for DSM-5: A developmentally informed assessment tool for trauma-exposed youth. *Journal of the American Academy of Child and Adolescent Psychiatry, 59*(1), 186–194. https://doi.org/10.1016/j.jaac.2018.10.019

Kaufman, E. A., Xia, M., Fosco, G., Yaptangco, M., Skidmore, C. R., Crowell, S. E. (2016). The Difficulties in Emotion Regulation Scale Short Form (DERS-SF): Validation and replication in adolescent and adult samples. *Journal of Psychopathology and Behavioral Assessment, 38*, 443–455. https://doi.org/10.1007/s10862-015-9529-3

Kelly, P. J., Owen, S. V., Peralez-Dieckmann, E., & Martinez, E. (2007). Health interventions with girls in the juvenile justice system. *Women's Health Issues, 17*(4), 227–236. https://doi.org/10.1016/j.whi.2007.03.005

Kim, Y. K., Yang, M. Y., Barthelemy, J. J., & Lofaso, B. M. (2018). A binary gender analysis to bullying, dating violence, and attempted suicide: The disproportionate effect of depression and psychological harm. *Children and Youth Services Review, 90*, 141–148. https://doi.org/10.1016/j.childyouth.2018.05.028

Kimble, M., Neacsiu, A. D., Flack, W. F., & Horner, J. (2008). Risk of unwanted sex for college women: Evidence for a red zone. *Journal of American College Health, 57*(3), 331–338. https://doi.org/10.3200/JACH.57.3.331-338

Langhinrichsen-Rohling, J., & Turner, L. A. (2012). The efficacy of an intimate partner violence prevention program with high-risk adolescent girls: A preliminary test. *Prevention Science, 13*(4), 384–394. https://doi.org/10.1007/s11121-011-0240-7

Levesque, D. A., Johnson, J. L., Welch, C. A., Prochaska, J. M., & Paiva, A. L. (2016). Teen dating violence prevention: Cluster-randomized trial of Teen Choices, an online, stage-based program for healthy, nonviolent relationships. *Psychology of Violence, 6*(3), 421–432. https://doi.org/10.1037/vio0000049

Linehan, M. M., (2014). *DBT training manual.* Guilford Press.

Maheux, A. J., Evans, R., Widman, L., Nesi, J., Prinstein, M. J., & Choukas-Bradley, S. (2020). Popular peer norms and adolescent sexting behavior. *Journal of Adolescence, 78*, 62–66. https://doi.org/10.1016/j.adolescence.2019.12.002

Manning, W. D., Longmore, M. A., Copp, J., & Giordano, P. C. (2014). The complexities of adolescent dating and sexual relationships: Fluidity, meaning (s), and implications for young adults' well-being. *New Directions for Child and Adolescent Development, 2014*(144), 53–69. https://doi.org/10.1002/cad.20060

Martin-Storey, A., Pollitt, A. M., & Baams, L. (2021). Profiles and predictors of dating violence among sexual and gender minority adolescents. *Journal of Adolescent Health, 68*(6), 1155–1161. https://doi.org/10.1016/j.jadohealth.2020.08.034

McCauley, H. L., Breslau, J. A., Saito, N., & Miller, E. (2015). Psychiatric disorders prior to dating initiation and physical dating violence before age 21: Findings from the National Comorbidity Survey Replication (NCS-R). *Social Psychiatry and Psychiatric Epidemiology, 50*, 1357–1365. https://doi.org/10.1007/s00127-015-1044-z

Mckee, A. C., & Daneshvar, D. H. (2015). The neuropathology of traumatic brain injury. *Handbook of Clinical Neurology, 127*, 45–66. https://doi.org/10.1016/B978-0-444-52892-6.00004-0

Meyers, J. R., & Schmidt, F. (2008). Predictive validity of the Structured Assessment for Violence Risk in Youth (SAVRY) with juvenile offenders. *Criminal Justice and Behavior, 35*(3), 344–355. https://doi.org/10.1177/0093854807311972

Miller, E., Goldstein, S., McCauley, H. L., Jones, K. A., Dick, R. N., Jetton, J., Silverman, J. G., Blackburn, S., Monasterio, E., James, L., & Tancredi, D. J. (2015). A school health center intervention for abusive adolescent relationships: A cluster RCT. *Pediatrics, 135*(1), 76–85. https://doi.org/10.1542/peds.2014-2471

Miller, E., Tancredi, D. J., McCauley, H. L., Decker, M. R., Virata, M. C. D., Anderson, H. A., Stetkevich, N., Brown, E. W., Moideen, F., Silverman, J. G. (2012). "Coaching boys into men": A cluster-randomized controlled trial of a dating violence prevention program. *Journal of Adolescent Health, 51*(5), 431–438. https://doi.org/10.1016/j.jadohealth.2012.01.018

Miller, S., Gorman-Smith, D., Sullivan, T., Orpinas, P., & Simon, T. R. (2009). Parent and peer predictors of physical dating violence perpetration in early adolescence: Tests of moderation and gender differences. *Journal of Clinical Child & Adolescent Psychology, 38*(4), 538–550. https://doi.org/10.1080/15374410902976270

Mpofu, J. J., Underwood, J. M., Thornton, J. E., Brener, N. D., Rico, A., Kilmer, G., Harris, W. A., Leon-Nguyen, M., Chyen, D., Lim, C., Mbaka, C. K., Smith-Grant, J., Whittle, L., Jones, S. E., Krause, K., Li, J., Shanklin, S. L., McKinnon, I., Arrey, L., Queen, B. E., & Roberts, A. M. (2023). *Overview and methods for the Youth Risk Behavior Surveillance System – United States, 2021. MMWR Supplements, 72*(1), 1–12.

Nahapetyan, L., Orpinas, P., Song, X., & Holland, K. (2014). Longitudinal association of suicidal ideation and physical dating violence among high school students. *Journal of Youth and Adolescence, 43*(4), 629–640. https://doi.org/10.1007/s10964-013-0006-6

Niolon, P. H., Vivolo-Kantor, A. M., Tracy, A. J., Latzman, N. E., Little, T. D., DeGue, S., Lang, K. M., Estefan, L. F., Ghazarian, S. R., McIntosh, W. L. K., Taylor, B., Johnson, L. J., Kuoh, H., Burton, T., Fortson, B., Mumford, E. A., Nelson, S. C., Joseph, H., Valle, L. A., & Tharp, A. T. (2019). An RCT of dating matters: Effects on teen dating violence and relationship behaviors. *American Journal of Preventive Medicine, 57*(1), 13–23.

Orchowski, L. M., Barnett, N. P., Berkowitz, A., Borsari, B., Oesterle, D., & Zlotnick, C. (2018). Sexual assault prevention for heavy drinking college men: Development and feasibility of an integrated approach. *Violence Against Women, 24*(11), 1369–1396. https://doi.org/10.1177/1077801218787928

Pagura, J., Stein, M. B., Bolton, J. M., Cox, B. J., Grant, B., & Sareen, J. (2010). Comorbidity of borderline personality disorder and posttraumatic stress disorder in the US population. *Journal of Psychiatric Research, 44*(16), 1190–1198. https://doi.org/10.1016/j.jpsychires.2010.04.016

Park, Y., Mulford, C., & Blachman-Demner, D. (2018). The acute and chronic impact of adolescent dating violence: A public health perspective. In D. A. Wolfe & J. R. Temple (Eds.), *Adolescent dating violence: Theory, research, and prevention* (pp. 53–83). Elsevier Academic Press. https://doi.org/10.1016/B978-0-12-811797-2.00003-7

Payne, D. L., Lonsway, K. A., & Fitzgerald, L. F. (1999). Rape myth acceptance: Exploration of its structure and its measurement using the Illinois rape myth acceptance scale. *Journal of Research in Personality, 33*(1), 27–68. https://doi.org/10.1006/jrpe.1998.2238

Peskin, M. F., Markham, C. M., Shegog, R., Baumler, E. R., Addy, R. C., Temple, J. R., Hernandez, B., Cuccaro, P. M., Thiel, M. A., Gabay, E. K., & Tortolero Emery, S. R. (2019). Adolescent Dating Violence Prevention Program for Early Adolescents: The Me & You Randomized Controlled Trial, 2014–2015. *American Journal of Public Health, 109*(10), 1419–1428. https://doi.org/10.2105/ajph.2019.305218

Pool, A. C., Patterson, F., Luna, I. Y., Hohl, B., & Bauer, K. W. (2017). Ten-year secular trends in youth violence: Results From the Philadelphia Youth Risk Behavior Survey 2003–2013. *Journal of School Health, 87*(4), 244–252. https://doi.org/10.1111/josh.12491

Porter, J., & Williams, L. M. (2011). Intimate violence among underrepresented groups on a college campus. *Journal of Interpersonal Violence, 26*(16), 3210–3224. https://doi.org/10.1177/0886260510393011

Prentky, R. A., & Righthand, S. (2003). *Juvenile Sex Offender Assessment Protocol-II (J-SOAP-II) manual.* US Department of Justice, Office of Justice Programs, Office of Juvenile Justice and Delinquency Prevention.

Price, E. L., Byers, E. S., Belliveau, N., Bonner, R., Caron, B., Doiron, D., Greenough, J., Guerette-Breau, A., Hicks, L., Landry, A., Lavoie, B., Layden-Oreto, M., Legere, L., Lemieux, S., Lirette, M., Maillet, G., McMullin, C., & Moore, R. (1999). The attitudes towards dating violence scales: Development and initial validation. *Journal of Family Violence, 14*, 351–375.

Pynoos, R. S., Weathers, F. W., Steinberg, A. M., Marx, B. P., Layne, C. M., Kaloupek, D. G., Schnurr, P. P., Keane, T. M., Blake, D. D., Newman, E., Nader, K. O., & Kriegler, J. A. (2015). *Clinician-Administered PTSD Scale for DSM-5 – Child/Adolescent Version.* National Center for PTSD. https://www.ptsd.va.gov/

Rancher, C., Jouriles, E. N., Rosenfield, D., Temple, J. R., & McDonald, R. (2019). The mediating role of trauma symptoms in the association between past and future teen dating violence victimization. *Journal of Abnormal Child Psychology, 47*, 475–485. https://doi.org/10.1007/s10802-018-0461-3

Rathus, J. H., & Miller, A. L. (2015). *DBT®skills manual for adolescents*. Guilford Press.

Resick, P. A., Monson, C. M., & Chard, K. M. (2016). *Cognitive processing therapy for PTSD: A comprehensive manual*. Guilford Press.

Reuter, T. R., Sharp, C., Temple, J. R., & Babcock, J. C. (2015). The relation between borderline personality disorder features and teen dating violence. *Psychology of Violence, 5*(2), 163–173. https://doi.org/10.1037/a0037891

Reyes, H. L. M., Foshee, V. A., Niolon, P. H., Reidy, D. E., & Hall, J. E. (2016). Gender role attitudes and male adolescent dating violence perpetration: Normative beliefs as moderators. *Journal of Youth and Adolescence, 45*, 350–360. https://doi.org/10.1007/s10964-015-0278-0

Reyes, H. L. M., Foshee, V. A., Tharp, A. T., Ennett, S. T., & Bauer, D. J. (2015). Substance use and physical dating violence: The role of contextual moderators. *American Journal of Preventive Medicine, 49*(3), 467–475. https://doi.org/10.1016/j.amepre.2015.05.018

Riggs, D. S., & O'Leary, K. D. (1989). A theoretical model of courtship aggression. In M. A. Pirog-Good & J. E. Stets (Eds.), *Violence in dating relationships: Emerging social issues* (pp. 53–71). Praeger.

Rizzo, C. J., Esposito-Smythers, C., Swenson, L., Hower, H. M., Wolff, J., & Spirito, A. (2014). Dating violence victimization, dispositional aggression, and nonsuicidal self-injury among psychiatrically hospitalized male and female adolescents. *Suicide and Life-Threatening Behavior, 44*(3), 338–351. https://doi.org/10.1111/sltb.12081

Rizzo, C. J., Joppa, M., Barker, D., Collibee, C., Zlotnick, C., & Brown, L. K. (2018). Project Date SMART: A dating violence (DV) and sexual risk prevention program for adolescent girls with prior DV exposure. *Prevention Science, 19*(4), 416–426. https://doi.org/10.1007/s11121-018-0871-z

Rothman, E. F. (2018). Theories on the causation of partner abuse perpetration. In D. A. Wolfe & J. R. Temple (Eds.), *Adolescent dating violence: Theory, research, and prevention* (pp. 25–51). Elsevier Academic Press. https://doi.org/10.1016/B978-0-12-811797-2.00002-5

Rothman, E. F., Paruk, J., Cuevas, C. A., Temple, J. R., & Gonzales, K. (2022). The development of the Measure of Adolescent Relationship Harassment and Abuse (MARSHA): Input from Black and multiracial, Latinx, Native American, and LGBTQ+ youth. *Journal of Interpersonal Violence, 37*(5-6), 2126–2149.

Rothman, E., & Silverman, J. (2007). The effect of a college sexual assault prevention program on first-year students' victimization rates. *Journal of American College Health, 55*(5), 283–290. https://doi.org/10.3200/JACH.55.5.283-290

Rothman, E. F., Stuart, G. L., Heeren, T., Paruk, J., & Bair-Merritt, M. (2020). The effects of a health Care-Based brief intervention on dating abuse perpetration: Results of a RCT. *Prevention Science, 21*(3), 366–376. https://doi.org/10.1007/s11121-019-01054-w

Rothman, E. F., & Xuan, Z. (2014). Trends in physical dating violence victimization among US high school students, 1999–2011. *Journal of School Violence, 13*(3), 277–290. https://doi.org/10.1080/15388220.2013.847377

Rowe, L. S., Jouriles, E. N., & McDonald, R. (2015). Reducing sexual victimization among adolescent girls: A randomized controlled pilot trial of My Voice, My Choice. *Behavior Therapy, 46*(3), 315–327. https://doi.org/10.1016/j.beth.2014.11.003

Russell, K. N., Voith, L. A., & Lee, H. (2021). Randomized controlled trials evaluating adolescent dating violence prevention programs with an outcome of reduced perpetration and/or victimization: A meta-analysis. *Journal of Adolescence, 87*(1), 6–14. https://doi.org/10.1016/j.adolescence.2020.12.009

Salazar, L. F., & Cook, S. L. (2006). Preliminary findings from an outcome evaluation of an intimate partner violence prevention program for adjudicated, African American, adolescent males. *Youth Violence and Juvenile Justice, 4*(4), 368–385. https://doi.org/10.1177/1541204006292818

Sargent, K. S., Jouriles, E. N., Rosenfield, D., & McDonald, R. (2017). A high school-based evaluation of TakeCARE, a video bystander program to prevent adolescent relationship violence. *Journal of Youth and Adolescence, 46*, 633–643. https://doi.org/10.1007/s10964-016-0622-z

Sargent, K. S., Krauss, A., Jouriles, E. N., & McDonald, R. (2016). Cyber victimization, psychological intimate partner violence, and problematic mental health outcomes among first-year college students. *Cyberpsychology, Behavior, and Social Networking, 19*(9), 545–550. https://doi.org/10.1089/cyber.2016.0115

Séguin, J. R. (2009). The frontal lobe and aggression. *European Journal of Developmental Psychology, 6*(1), 100–119.

Shorey, R. C., Cohen, J. R., Lu, Y., Fite, P. J., Stuart, G. L., & Temple, J. R. (2017). Age of onset for physical and sexual teen dating violence perpetration: A longitudinal investigation. *Preventive Medicine, 105*, 275–279. https://doi.org/10.1016/j.ypmed.2017.10.008

Shorey, R. C., Fite, P. J., Cohen, J. R., Stuart, G. L., & Temple, J. R. (2018). The stability of intimate partner violence perpetration from adolescence to emerging adulthood in sexual minorities. *Journal of Adolescent Health, 62*(6), 747–749. https://doi.org/10.1016/j.jadohealth.2017.11.307

Singh, V., Epstein-Ngo, Q., Cunningham, R. M., Stoddard, S. A., Chermack, S. T., & Walton, M. A. (2015). Physical dating violence among adolescents and young adults with alcohol misuse. *Drug and Alcohol Dependence, 153*, 364–368. https://doi.org/10.1016/j.drugalcdep.2015.05.003

Slep, A. M. S., Cascardi, M., Avery-Leaf, S., & O'Leary, K. D. (2001). Two new measures of attitudes about the acceptability of teen dating aggression. *Psychological Assessment, 13*(3), 306–318.

Smith, D. M., & Donnelly, J. (2000). Adolescent dating violence: A multi-systemic approach of enhancing awareness in educators, parents, and society. *Journal of Prevention & Intervention in the Community, 21*(1), 53–64. https://doi.org/10.1300/J005v21n01_04

Smith, S. G., Zhang, X., Basile, K. C., Merrick, M. T., Wang, J., Kresnow, M., & Chen, J. (2018). *The National Intimate Partner and Sexual Violence Survey: 2015 data brief – updated release.* Centers for Disease Control and Prevention.

Sobsey, D., Wells, D., Lucardic, R., & Mansell, S. (1995). *Violence and disability: An annotated bibliography.* Brookes.

Spencer, C. M., Anders, K. M., Toews, M. L., & Emanuels, S. K. (2020). Risk markers for physical teen dating violence victimization in the United States: A meta-analysis. *Journal of Youth and Adolescence, 49*, 575–589. https://doi.org/10.1007/s10964-020-01194-1

Spencer, C. M., Toews, M. L., Anders, K. M., & Emanuels, S. K. (2021). Risk markers for physical teen dating violence perpetration: A meta-analysis. *Trauma, Violence, & Abuse, 22*(3), 619–631. https://doi.org/10.1177/1524838019875700

Spielberger, C. D. (1999). *STAXI-2: State-Trait Anger Expression Inventory-2.* Psychological Assessment Resources.

Straus, M. A., Hamby, S. L., Boney-McCoy, S. U. E., & Sugarman, D. B. (1996). The revised Conflict Tactics Scales (CTS2) development and preliminary psychometric data. *Journal of Family Issues, 17*(3), 283–316. https://doi.org/10.1177/019251396017003001

Straussner, S. L. A., & Calnan, A. J. (2014). Trauma through the life cycle: A review of current literature. *Clinical Social Work Journal, 42*, 323–335. https://doi.org/10.1007/s10615-014-0496-z

Tator, C. H. (2013). Concussions and their consequences: Current diagnosis, management and prevention. *Canadian Medical Association Journal, 185*(11), 975–979. https://doi.org/10.1503/cmaj.120039

Taylor, B. G., & Mumford, E. A. (2016). A national descriptive portrait of adolescent relationship abuse: Results from the national survey on teen relationships and intimate violence. *Journal of Interpersonal Violence, 31*(6), 963–988. https://doi.org/10.1177/0886260514564070

Taylor, B., Stein, N. D., Woods, D., & Mumford, E. (2011). *Shifting boundaries: Final report on an experimental evaluation of a youth dating violence prevention program in New York City middle schools.* https://www.ojp.gov/pdffiles1/nij/grants/236175.pdf

Temple, J. R., Baumler, E., Wood, L., Franco, K. S., Peskin, M., & Shumate C. (2024). Cumulative incidence of physical and sexual dating violence: Results from a long-term longitudinal study. *Journal of Interpersonal Violence, 39,* 734–755. https://doi.org/10.1177/08862605231200218

Temple, J. R., Baumler, E., Wood, L., Thiel, M., Peskin, M., & Torres, E. (2021). A dating violence prevention program for middle school youth: A cluster randomized trial. *Pediatrics, 148*(5), e2021052880. https://doi.org/10.1542/peds.2021-052880

Temple, J. R., Choi, H. J., Brem, M., Wolford-Clevenger, C., Stuart, G. L., Peskin, M. F., & Elmquist, J. (2016). The temporal association between traditional and cyber dating abuse among adolescents. *Journal of Youth and Adolescence, 45,* 340–349. https://doi.org/10.1007/s10964-015-0380-3

Temple, J. R., Shorey, R. C., Fite, P., Stuart, G. L., & Le, V. D. (2013). Substance use as a longitudinal predictor of the perpetration of teen dating violence. *Journal of Youth and Adolescence, 42,* 596–606. https://doi.org/10.1007/s10964-012-9877-1

Temple, J. R., Weston, R., & Marshall, L. L. (2005). Physical and mental health outcomes of women in nonviolent, unilaterally violent, and mutually violent relationships. *Violence and Victims, 20*(3), 335–359. https://doi.org/10.1891/vivi.20.3.335

Terrazas-Carrillo, E., Garcia, E., Vasquez, D. A., Sabina, C., & Rodriguez, A. S. (2021). DRIVEN to change attitudes toward dating violence: Outcomes from a 6-month follow-up study. *Journal of Prevention and Health Promotion, 2*(2), 311–328. https://doi.org/10.1177/26320770211039158

Tharp, A. T., McNaughton Reyes, H. L., Foshee, V., Swahn, M. H., Hall, J. E., & Logan, J. (2017). Examining the prevalence and predictors of injury from adolescent dating violence. *Journal of Aggression, Maltreatment & Trauma, 26*(5), 445–461. https://doi.org/10.1080/10926771.2017.1287145

US Census Bureau. (2022). *National Population by Characteristics: 2020–2021. Annual estimates of the resident population by single year of age and sex for the United States: April 1, 2020 to July 1, 2021.* https://census.gov/data/datasets/time-series/demo/popest/2020s-national-detail.html

US Centers for Disease Control and Prevention. (2024). *About the public health approach to violence prevention.* https://www.cdc.gov/violence-prevention/about/about-the-public-health-approach-to-violence-prevention.html?CDC_AAref_Val=https://www.cdc.gov/violenceprevention/about/publichealthapproach.html

US Department of Education. (2019). *Chronic absenteeism in the nation's schools: A hidden educational crisis.*

Vagi, K. J., Olsen, E. O. M., Basile, K. C., & Vivolo-Kantor, A. M. (2015). Teen dating violence (physical and sexual) among US high school students: Findings from the 2013 National Youth Risk Behavior Survey. *JAMA Pediatrics, 169*(5), 474–482. https://doi.org/10.1001/jamapediatrics.2014.3577

Vagi, K. J., Rothman, E. F., Latzman, N. E., Tharp, A. T., Hall, D. M., & Breiding, M. J. (2013). Beyond correlates: A review of risk and protective factors for adolescent dating violence perpetration. *Journal of Youth and Adolescence, 42,* 633–649. https://doi.org/10.1007/s10964-013-9907-7

Walker, K., Bowen, E., & Brown, S. (2013). Psychological and criminological factors associated with desistance from violence: A review of the literature. *Aggression and Violent Behavior, 18*(2), 286–299. https://doi.org/10.1016/j.avb.2012.11.021

Walker, L. E. (2016). *The battered woman syndrome* (4th ed.). Springer Publishing.

Widom, C. S., Dutton, M. A., Czaja, S. J., & DuMont, K. A. (2005). Development and validation of a new instrument to assess lifetime trauma and victimization history. *Journal of Traumatic Stress, 18*(5), 519–531. https://doi.org/10.1002/jts.20060

Wolfe, D. A., Crooks, C. V., Chiodo, D., Hughes, R., & Ellis, W. (2012). Observations of adolescent peer resistance skills following a classroom-based healthy relationship program: A post-intervention comparison. *Prevention Science, 13*(2):196–205.

Wolfe, D. A., Crooks, C., Jaffe, P., Chiodo, D., Hughes, R., Ellis, W., Stitt, L., Donner, A. (2009). A school-based program to prevent adolescent dating violence: A cluster randomized trial. *Archives of Pediatrics & Adolescent Medicine, 163*(8), 692–699. https://doi.org/10.1001/archpediatrics.2009.69

Wolfe, D. A., Scott, K., Reitzel-Jaffe, D., Wekerle, C., Grasley, C., & Straatman, A. L. (2001). Development and validation of the conflict in adolescent dating relationships inventory. *Psychological Assessment, 13*(2), 277. https://doi.org/10.1037/1040-3590.13.2.277

Wong, J. S., Bouchard, J., & Lee, C. (2023). The effectiveness of college dating violence prevention programs: A meta-analysis. *Trauma, Violence & Abuse, 24*(2), 684–701. https://doi.org/10.1177/15248380211036058

Woodin, E. M., & O'Leary, K. D. (2010). A brief motivational intervention for physically aggressive dating couples. *Prevention Science, 11*(4), 371–383.

World Health Organization. (2022). *International Classification of Diseases, 11th Revision* (ICD-11).

Worling, J. R. (2017). *PROFESOR: Protective + Risk Observations For Eliminating Sexual Offense Recidivism.* https://www.profesor.ca/

Ybarra, M. L., Espelage, D. L., Langhinrichsen-Rohling, J., Korchmaros, J. D., & Boyd, D. (2016). Lifetime prevalence rates and overlap of physical, psychological, and sexual dating abuse perpetration and victimization in a national sample of youth. *Archives of Sexual Behavior, 45*, 1083–1099. https://doi.org/10.1007/s10508-016-0748-9

Zweig, J. M., Dank, M., Yahner, J., & Lachman, P. (2013). The rate of cyber dating abuse among teens and how it relates to other forms of teen dating violence. *Journal of Youth and Adolescence, 42*(7), 1063–1077. https://doi.org/10.1007/s10964-013-9922-8.

8

Appendix: Tools and Resources

The following materials for your book can be downloaded free of charge once you register on the Hogrefe website.

Appendix 1: Measure of Adolescent Relationship Harassment and Abuse (MARSHA) – Victimization and Perpetration Version

Appendix 2: Measure of Adolescent Relationship Harassment and Abuse (MARSHA) SHORT FORM – MARSHA-SF

Appendix 3: Measure of Adolescent Relationship Harassment and Abuse (MARSHA) – 3-Item Screener

How to proceed:

1. Go to www.hgf.io/media and create a user account. If you already have one, please log in.

2. Go to **My supplementary materials** in your account dashboard and enter the code below. You will automatically be redirected to the download area, where you can access and download the supplementary materials.

   Code: B-LHUXBB

To make sure you have permanent direct access to all the materials, we recommend that you download them and save them on your computer.

Appendix 1: <u>M</u>easure of <u>A</u>dolescent <u>R</u>elation<u>s</u>hip <u>H</u>arassment and <u>A</u>buse (MARSHA) – Victimization and Perpetration Version

This is a **preview** of the content that is available in the downloadable material of this book. Please see p. 86 for instructions on how to obtain the full-sized, printable PDF.

Instructions: Think about all of the people you were *dating, hooking up with, or in a romantic relationship within the past year*. Answer the following questions thinking about these people. How many times did the following things happen, *not for fun or as a joke*? Your best guess about the number of times is OK.

	0 times	1–3 times	4–10 times	More than 10 times
1. They looked through my phone or other device at my texts, social media, or apps, when I did not want them to do that.	0	1	2	3
2. I looked through their phone or other device at their texts, social media, or apps, when they did not know I was doing that or they did not want me to do that.	0	1	2	3
3. They used social media or other apps to keep track of me or monitor where I was going or where I had been.	0	1	2	3
4. I used social media or other apps to keep track of them and monitor where they were going or where they had been.	0	1	2	3
5. They asked me to show them things on my phone or other device, such as texts or social media.	0	1	2	3
6. I asked them to show me things on their phone or other device, such as texts or social media.	0	1	2	3
7. They asked me to give them one or more of my passwords.	0	1	2	3
8. I asked them to give me one or more of their passwords.	0	1	2	3
9. They messaged me constantly and I felt like they were keeping track of me or monitoring what I was doing.	0	1	2	3
10. I messaged them constantly in order to keep track of them or monitor what they were doing.	0	1	2	3
11. They changed my passwords in order to lock me out of my own phone, computer, other device, social media, or other online accounts.	0	1	2	3
12. I changed their passwords in order to lock them out of their own phone, computer, other device, social media or other online accounts.	0	1	2	3
13. They tried to stop me from spending time with my family or friends.	0	1	2	3
14. I tried to stop them from spending time with their family or friends.	0	1	2	3
15. They tried to go with me when I was doing something with my family or friends, even when I didn't want them to join.	0	1	2	3
16. I tried to go with them when they were doing something with their friends or family, even when they might not have wanted me to join.	0	1	2	3
17. They made me feel like I could not break up with them or get out of the relationship.	0	1	2	3
18. I tried to make them feel like they could not break up with me or get out of the relationship.	0	1	2	3

	0 times	1–3 times	4–10 times	More than 10 times
19. They followed me or spied on me or stalked me in real life (not online).	0	1	2	3
20. I followed them or spied on them, or stalked them in real life (not online).	0	1	2	3
21. I sent them scary or threatening messages via text, social media, or another app.**	0	1	2	3
22. They demanded that I spend money on them even if I didn't want to.	0	1	2	3
23. I demanded that they spend money on me even if they didn't want to.	0	1	2	3
24. I made them give me money.**	0	1	2	3
25. They spread rumors, gossip, or secrets about me using texts, social media, or apps.	0	1	2	3
26. I spread rumors, gossip, or secrets about them using texts, social media, or apps.	0	1	2	3
27. They threatened to, or actually, spread rumors about me.	0	1	2	3
28. I threatened to, or actually spread, rumors about them.	0	1	2	3
29. They tried to get their friends to stop talking to me or stop being friends with me.	0	1	2	3
30. I tried to get their friends to stop talking to them or stop being friends with them.	0	1	2	3
31. They insulted my family, culture, race, ethnicity, sexual orientation, gender, or religion, and it made me feel bad, embarrassed, or insecure.	0	1	2	3
32. I insulted their family, culture, race, ethnicity, sexual orientation, gender identity or religion, to make them feel bad, embarrassed, or insecure.	0	1	2	3
33. They insulted my looks, clothes, or appearance, and it made me feel bad, embarrassed, or insecure.	0	1	2	3
34. I insulted their looks, clothes, or appearance, to make them feel bad, embarrassed, or insecure.	0	1	2	3
35. They used technology in some other way that made me feel scared, humiliated, embarrassed, threatened, or harassed.*	0	1	2	3
36. They used a stick, bat, or some other weapon on me.	0	1	2	3
37. I used a stick, bat, or some other weapon on them.	0	1	2	3
38. They used a gun or knife on me.	0	1	2	3
39. I used a gun or knife on them.	0	1	2	3
40. I damaged their property or belongings on purpose.**	0	1	2	3
41. They slapped, pushed, shoved, or shook me.	0	1	2	3
42. I slapped, pushed, shoved, or shook them.	0	1	2	3
43. They hit, punched, kicked, or choked me.	0	1	2	3
44. I hit, punched, kicked, or choked them.	0	1	2	3

This is a **preview** of the content that is available in the downloadable material of this book. Please see p. 86 for instructions on how to obtain the full-sized, printable PDF.

	0 times	1–3 times	4–10 times	More than 10 times
45. They got other people to hit me or beat me up.	0	1	2	3
46. I got other people to hit them or beat them up.	0	1	2	3
47. They did something to cause me a bruise, cut, scratch, burn, sprain, or other injury.	0	1	2	3
48. I did something to them to cause a bruise, cut, scratch, burn, sprain, or other injury.	0	1	2	3
49. They threatened to, or actually hurt, someone I care about.	0	1	2	3
50. I threatened to, or actually hurt, someone they care about.	0	1	2	3
51. They pressured me to do something sexual.	0	1	2	3
52. I pressured them to do something sexual.	0	1	2	3
53. They asked or pressured me for a nude or almost nude photo or video of me, when I did not want to give them one.	0	1	2	3
54. I asked, or pressured them, for a nude or almost nude photo or video of themselves, when they might not have wanted to give me one.	0	1	2	3
55. They forced or pressured me to take nude or almost nude photos or videos.	0	1	2	3
56. I forced or pressured them to take nude or almost nude photos or videos.	0	1	2	3
57. They forced me to do something sexual.	0	1	2	3
58. I forced them to do something sexual.	0	1	2	3
59. They gave me alcohol or drugs in order to get sexual with me when I did not want to get sexual.	0	1	2	3
60. I gave them alcohol or drugs in order to get sexual with them because they might not have wanted to get sexual.	0	1	2	3
61. They showed or sent other people nude, or almost nude, photos or videos of me and I did not want them to do that.	0	1	2	3
62. I showed or sent other people nude or almost nude photos or videos of them that they didn't know about or might not have wanted me to do.	0	1	2	3
63. They yelled, screamed, or swore at me.	0	1	2	3
64. I yelled, screamed, or swore at them.	0	1	2	3
65. They punched the wall, slammed the door, or threw something.	0	1	2	3
66. I punched the wall, slammed the door, or threw something.	0	1	2	3
67. They threatened to hit me, which scared or worried me.	0	1	2	3
68. I threatened to hit them to scare or worry them.	0	1	2	3
69. They stopped talking to me and I felt punished, hurt, or scared.	0	1	2	3
70. I stopped talking to them to punish, hurt, or scare them.	0	1	2	3
71. I told them that I was cheating on them, even if I wasn't, just to make them feel bad.**	0	1	2	3

This is a **preview** of the content that is available in the downloadable material of this book. Please see p. 86 for instructions on how to obtain the full-sized, printable PDF.

	0 times	1–3 times	4–10 times	More than 10 times
Supplemental Questions (ages 16–21)				
S1v They didn't let me use birth control or use condoms in the way we agreed on (such as, didn't use a condom, messed with birth control pills).	0	1	2	3
S1p I didn't use birth control or use condoms in the way we agreed on (such as, didn't use a condom, messed with birth control pills).	0	1	2	3
S2v They tried to make me pregnant, or pressured me to get pregnant.	0	1	2	3
S2p I tried to get them pregnant, or pressured them to get pregnant.	0	1	2	3
S3v They locked me out of my house or apartment.	0	1	2	3
S3p I locked them out of their house or apartment.	0	1	2	3

Note. * Only asked for victimization, no perpetration version. ** Only asked for perpetration, no victimization version

Further reading:

Rothman, E. F., Paruk, J., Cuevas, C. A., Temple, J., & Gonzales, K. (2020). The development of the Measure of Adolescent Relationship Harassment and Abuse (MARSHA): Input from Black and Multiracial, Latinx, Native American, and LGBTQ+ youth. *Journal of Interpersonal Violence*, *37*(5–6), 2126–2149. https://doi.org/10.1177/0886260520936367

Rothman, E. F., Cuevas, C. A., Mumford, E., Bahrami, E., & Taylor, B. (2021). The psychometric properties of the Measure of Adolescent Relationship Harassment and Abuse (MARSHA) with a nationally representative sample of U.S. youth. *Journal of Interpersonal Violence*, 37(11–12), NP9714–NP9737. https://doi.org/10.1177/0886260520985480

Subscales:

Victimization, Privacy control: Questions 1, 3, 5, 7, 9, 11, 13, 15, 17, 19
Victimization, Social control: Questions 22, 25, 27, 29, 31, 33, 35
Victimization, Physical abuse: Questions 36, 38, 41, 43, 45, 47, 49
Victimization, Sexual abuse: Questions 51, 53, 55, 57, 59, 61
Victimization, Intimidation: Questions 63, 65, 67, 69
Perpetration, Social control: Questions 23, 24, 26, 28, 30, 32, 34, 50, 71
Perpetration, Physical abuse: Questions 37, 39, 40, 42, 44, 46, 48
Perpetration, Sexual abuse: Questions 52, 54, 56, 58, 60, 62
Perpetration, Isolation: Questions 10, 14, 16, 18, 20, 21
Perpetration, Cyber Control: Questions 2, 4, 6, 8, 12
Perpetration, Intimidation: Questions 64, 66, 68, 70

Scoring: Add points for each item (0 to 3) to create a total scale score for victimization and perpetration as well as the score for each subscale.

If a respondent skipped two more items for any of the subscales, that subscale should not be scored and considered incomplete. If a total of 10 or more questions are skipped in the victimization or perpetration questions, then the full MARSHA for victimization or perpetration should be considered incomplete.

A score of 0 means no dating abuse or unhealthy relationship behavior.

A score of 1 and higher indicates the presence of unhealthy relationship behavior experience. Higher scores indicate greater frequency of unhealthy relationship behavior experiences.

Supplemental questions are added only on participants ages 16–21, however they should not be included in the final score if comparing to younger participant scores.

This is a **preview** of the content that is available in the downloadable material of this book. Please see p. 86 for instructions on how to obtain the full-sized, printable PDF.

Appendix 2: <u>M</u>easure of <u>A</u>dolescent <u>R</u>elationship <u>H</u>arassment and <u>A</u>buse (MARSHA) SHORT FORM – MARSHA-SF

This is a **preview** of the content that is available in the downloadable material of this book. Please see p. 86 for instructions on how to obtain the full-sized, printable PDF.

Instructions: Think about all of the people you were *dating, hooking up with, or in a romantic relationship within the past year*. Answer the following questions thinking about these people. Did the following things happen, *not for fun or as a joke?*

Victimization items		
1. They slapped, pushed, shoved or shook me.	Yes	No
2. They hit, punched, kicked or choked me.	Yes	No
3. They asked or pressured me for a nude or almost nude photo or video of me, when I did not want to give them one.	Yes	No
4. They yelled, screamed or swore at me	Yes	No
5. They punched the wall, slammed the door, or threw something.	Yes	No
6. They threatened to hit me, which scared or worried me.	Yes	No
7. They made me feel like I could not break up with them or get out of the relationship.	Yes	No
Perpetration items		
8. I slapped, pushed, shoved or shook them.	Yes	No
9. I hit, punched, kicked or choked them.	Yes	No
10. I asked, or pressured them, for a nude or almost nude photo or video of themselves, when they might not have wanted to give me one.	Yes	No
11. I yelled, screamed, or swore at them.	Yes	No
12. I punched the wall, slammed the door, or threw something.	Yes	No
13. I threatened to hit them to scare or worry them.	Yes	No
14. I tried to make them feel like they could not break up with me or get out of the relationship.	Yes	No

Further reading:

Paruk, J., Lancaster, C., & Rothman, E. F. (2005). *A short form of the Measure of Adolescent Relationship Harassment and Abuse (MARSHA-SF)* [Submitted for publication].

Scoring: Add 1 point for each YES response. Respondents will have a total score in the range of 0 to 7.

Appendix 3: <u>M</u>easure of <u>A</u>dolescent <u>R</u>elation<u>s</u>hip <u>H</u>arassment and <u>A</u>buse (MARSHA) – 3-Item Screener

This is a **preview** of the content that is available in the downloadable material of this book. Please see p. 86 for instructions on how to obtain the full-sized, printable PDF.

Instructions: Think about all of the people you were *dating, hooking up with, or in a romantic relationship within the past year.* Answer the following questions thinking about these people. Did the following things happen, *not for fun or as a joke?*

1. They yelled, screamed or swore at me.	Yes	No
2. They asked or pressured me for a nude or almost nude photo or video of me, when I did not want to give them one.	Yes	No
3. They made me feel like I could not break up with them or get out of the relationship.	Yes	No

Further reading:

Rothman, E. F., Campbell, J. K., Hoch, A. M., Bair-Merritt, M., Cuevas, C. A., Taylor, B., & Mumford, E. A. (2022). Validity of a three-item dating abuse victimization screening tool in a 11–21 year old sample. *BMC Pediatrics, 22,* Article 337. https://doi.org/10.1186/s12887-022-03397-w

Scoring: Add 1 point for each YES response. Respondents will have a total score in the range of 0 to 3.

A score of 1 or more means that there is 91% probability that the individual has experienced psychological, physical, sexual, or cyber dating abuse victimization in the past year.

Advances in Psychotherapy – Evidence-Based Practice

Developed and edited with the support of the Society of Clinical Psychology (APA Division 12)

Series editors

J. Kim Penberthy, PhD, ABPP
Heather Bruschwein, PsyD, ABPP
Jonathan S. Comer, PhD
Damion Grasso, PhD
Sarah Meshberg-Cohen, PhD
Jonathan Weinand, PhD

- *Practice-oriented*
- *Evidence-based*
- *Expert authors*
- *Easy-to-read*
- *Compact*
- *Cost-effective*

Latest releases

Volume 31, 2nd ed.   Volume 12, 2nd ed.   Volume 55   Volume 54

www.hogrefe.com/apt